The Three Ways of
Getting Things Done

*Hierarchy, Heterarchy & Responsible
Autonomy in Organizations*

Gerard Fairtlough

International Edition

With a foreword by Stewart Clegg

Published by:

Triarchy Press
Station Offices
Station Yard
Axminster EX13 5PF
United Kingdom

+44 (0)1297 631456

info@triarchypress.com
www.triarchypress.com

First Published 2005

International Edition 2007

A catalogue record for this book is available from the British Library.

Original cover photograph by Adrian Warren.

ISBN: 978-0-9550081-3-9

Acknowledgements

The thoughts that led to this book were stimulated by my membership of the Global Business Network (Emeryville, California) and particularly by the superb ideas of Jay Ogilvy and the late Donald Michael. Equally important were my involvement over several years with Professor Eve Mitleton-Kelly's Complexity Project at the London School of Economics, numerous discussions with Dr. John Gray of the University of Western Sydney and, more recently, discussions with Rosie Beckham. I thank them all.

I am grateful to Lisa Fairtlough, Arie de Geus, Jane Grant and Barbara Heinzen for valuable discussions and to Napier Collyns for continuing encouragement. I am also grateful to the organizers of seminars at which I presented my ideas on hierarchy and its alternatives. I learned a lot from the energetic feedback at these. The seminars included those at the LSE Complexity Project, the Don Michael Prize Award, Meridian, Innogen and Karen Otazo's elegant salon.

I first came across the term 'getting things done' when I worked with the Coverdale Organization. Raymond Williams's book 'Keywords' (Williams 1976) was particularly helpful to me when I was preparing the Glossary.

Thanks to Rosie Beckham for her superb bibliographic, research and design work on the project.

Contents

Foreword

Gerard Fairtlough is a rare type of individual; he has both been a major player in organizing corporate life and has made major contributions to the analysis of organizations. Some people have done the former and have written about their experiences; with few exceptions their books have little of value to bring to the scholarly community. Most corporate leaders' publications contributing to knowledge after corporate life conform more to the requirements of a heroic genre than they contribute to the body of research knowledge about organizations. Gerard Fairtlough is different; he is one of the very few individuals who have experienced at first hand the complexities of running both major corporate organizations and highly innovative start-ups. Fairtlough is a biochemist who worked in the Royal Dutch/Shell group for 25 years, the last five as CEO of Shell Chemicals UK. He then founded one of the UK's first major biotechnology companies, Celltech, and was its CEO for 10 years until 1990.

I first became aware of Gerard Fairtlough's work when a publisher asked me to read a manuscript that he had submitted for publication. He did not publish with that company, a university press of some distinction, despite my recommending acceptance, but chose an alternative company that would hasten the time to market. The book in question was 'Creative Compartments: A Design for Future Organization'[1]. It was an impressive book, showing not only a considerable grasp of organization theory but also a sophisticated understanding of social theory blended through the wisdom of someone who might have been the very model for Schön's reflective practitioner[2]. A corporate chieftain familiar with Habermas and Weber; moreover, one who was able to apply insights derived from reflection on these and other writers

---

1 Fairtlough, G. *Creative Compartments: A Design for Future Organization.* London: Adamantine Press, 1994.
2 Schön, D. A. *The Reflective Practitioner: How professionals think in action.* New York: Basic, 1983.

that many Business School colleagues would deem 'difficult' – this was an encounter with a mind that was rare!

The argument of the book was, in many ways, an anticipation of the scholarly programme now known as Positive Organizational Scholarship. In a nutshell, the thesis was that organizations that adopted elements of what Fairtlough called 'creative compartments' (an idea he took from his own discipline of biochemistry) would be characterized by complete openness about all task-related matters as well as considerable openness about personal matters: an openness which would generate enhanced levels of trust among all members of the compartment's community. Members of the compartment would thus develop a common culture and share a common language, with a common set of concepts, which would develop as communicative and problem-solving tools. Most communication within the compartment would be broadcast, open and uncodified. Within the compartment, members would hold strikingly different expectations about openness, trust, shared purposes and shared language compared with expectations across the boundary. It was a structure that would enhance innovation, creative problem-solving and adaptability to environmental change. Intense internal communication allows projects to be brought to fruition in a timely way, enables new projects to start easily, enhances performance standards and raises levels of quality.

It was an analysis that, sometime later, was to become much more existentially real for me as I was fortunate enough to be involved with something that was clearly a creative compartment: it was the Alliance Team designed to deliver a major piece of infrastructure for the Sydney 2000 Olympics, on the Northside Storage Tunnel Project. What was striking for the researchers on that project was the sheer sense of innovation and exhilaration that being in a creative compartment generated for the members of the project team: people assembled from diverse organizations in the Alliance, but with an overwhelming commitment to 'whatever was best for project'[3].

One striking thing about the Alliance was the lack of hierarchy. The organization structures and strictures of the members' respective organizations were left outside the Alliance. The leadership team rotated all roles and innovation was as likely to occur in a tool-box meeting on the tunnel floor as in the Alliance offices.

Now, in his latest book, Fairtlough demonstrates what is wrong with hierarchy – the conventional way of getting things done with command and control and bosses – and suggests that there are alternatives to hierarchy that we should take seriously. Hierarchy is what made Shell tick when he first worked there. As CEO he was expected to be an all-knowing autocrat, a ritualistic dictator, dispensing orders, steering the leviathan. At the same time he realized that he didn't know enough to tell other people what to do. Much better than the chief executive dictating, he thought, was a chance to talk to people throughout the organization, deliberately sharing views with each other to arrive at jointly held agreement and consensus. Such an approach is what characterized the Alliance that I and my colleagues researched and comprises the second of Gerard's three ways of getting things done: heterarchy, meaning multiple or dispersed rule rather than the singular rule one finds in hierarchy. Hierarchy is the default setting for the vast majority of organizations, ever since Max Weber articulated the organizational qualities of bureaucracy, which made the German state and military such a formidable machine under Bismarck, and which spread rapidly in a fast industrializing world – not

---

3   Reported in Pitsis, T., Clegg., S. R, Marosszeky, M. and Rura-Polley, T. (2003.) 'Constructing the Olympic Dream: Managing Innovation through the Future Perfect', *Organization Science*, 14:5, 574-590, and in Clegg, S. R., Pitsis, T., Rura-Polley T. and Marosszeky, M. (2002.) 'Governmentality Matters: Designing an Alliance Culture of Inter-organizational Collaboration for Managing Projects', *Organization Studies*, 23:3, 317-337.

least in the United States, where the Wharton School – the first business school – imported many current ideas from late nineteenth century Germany. These found their way into practice through the respect that the stewards of West Point held for Germany's formidable military accomplishments. The Wharton School adapted many ideas into its curriculum from the engineering community associated with institutions such as West Point and with the extensive civilian contracting its graduates did on the railways. Other famous engineering schools did the same, such as Rennselaer, Rochester, MIT, and the Stevens Institute of Technology, where F W Taylor gained his part-time degree. These military antecedents were, above all, the source of the default setting for hierarchy. Subsequently, in the terms that sociologists of organizations have adopted, it was imitation that became the primary mechanism of diffusion. Other organizations seeking to emulate the culturally imprinted properties of esteem and distinction, which ensured the normalcy of hierarchy, copied the form, creating institutional isomorphism, whether they did so through voluntary mimesis, coercive enforcement or normative desire.

Fairtlough identifies a third way of getting things done, responsible autonomy, which is self-government for an agreed purpose. It is a mode of organization that characterizes partnerships of professional services firms embracing accountants, lawyers and consultants. Responsible autonomy enables encapsulated boundedness to be created – with devices and agents for boundary spanning – thus extending functional capabilities. Of course, the establishment of efficient responsible autonomy means critique must be in place from the start; the rules and accountabilities need to be clear, and dispute resolution mechanisms must be created.

As Fairtlough states, the alternative to hierarchy is not chaos or anarchy. Only our powerful addiction to hierarchy, bred in habit, leads us to believe it to be so. And it is a 'powerful' addiction in a double sense; first, it is strong, and second, it is obfuscatory, because it creates blind spots, absences and silences where critical reflection should be. In the absence of critical reflection, alternatives are not thinkable; where there is critical reflection then alternatives become visible. Hierarchical rights, interpreted through a traditional conception, presume an established order of domination in which is vested a *repressive* right to exercise power over subjects.

Hierarchy has useful functions. It can be used to settle disputes unilaterally as disparate views are rejected in favour of hierarchically preferred options. But the risk is that it will produce stifling cultures of orthodoxy; structures which cannot easily learn from the diversity of their component strengths and voices; leaders who believe their own rhetoric rather than trust that wisdom might possibly reside in the views of those whom they seek to rule, sell to, supply and employ; and power which can only understand resistance to it in terms of illegitimate choices of illegitimate ways to express being an organization member. In shorthand, being a member, it is assumed, means being someone who accepts that the terms of trade for receipt of a wage or salary are that one keeps one's opinions to oneself where they conflict with those of authorities; that one's daily bread buys one's daily acquiescence to whatever authorities choose to do.

Hierarchy has many celebrated advantages, not least being familiarity, unity of powers and a theory of sovereignty that few would criticize openly. After all, we all know that what bosses do is rule. And the whole legal framework of common law, derived from Masters and Servants Acts, assumes definite powers distributed differentially in terms of relations built into the hierarchy. Little wonder that hierarchy is so normalized, so hegemonic, so deeply embedded legally. Within the limits of legal frameworks, those in dominant relations of hierarchy can do drastically bad things to the immediate life chances of those of us who are not - such as making us redundant. That is why, in an analysis of any system of power relations, one should never stop at the organization door, looking only at what goes on inside the organization. One also needs to consider the changing balance of forces in the industrial relations arena, as political parties of differing ideological persuasions use government to shift the balance of power between labour and capital over the legal definitions of what constitutes a contract of employment and its breaches. Often, the balance of power intra-organizationally changes dramatically as a result of changes registered in the political arena. Rights, such as to strike, to dismiss, to enjoy parental leave or statutory entitlement, ebb and flow with shifts of the political current, as does resistance to their creation, preservation, extension or erosion. Moving in one direction they embolden employers; shifting to another they create anxiety when they offer succour to employees, at what seems to employers to be their expense.

The paradigm of a sovereign master and commander is almost second nature. It provides an implicit and pervasive model of sovereignty for all strong, macho, business leaders. However, there are alternative definitions of sovereignty, significantly different from the paradigm of master and commander, which acknowledge *demos* and *poly* – democracy and polyarchy – as well as hierarchy and bureaucracy.

Fairtlough suggests that we simply do not know how desirable hierarchy is in particular situations, because it never gets tested against anything other than anarchy or chaos. What it should be tested against, Fairtlough suggests, are models of heterarchy and responsible autonomy. Heterarchy means the separation of powers; it builds sovereignty into practice rather than the precedent of domination. It sets up, at best, internal systems for the exercise of voice, the calling to account and the checking of power, whilst encouraging co-evolutionary learning because each party has to pay close attention to the cues and signals that the others are attending to; it cannot simply impose 'one best way' or 'my way or the highway' on members. It works from a team basis, enabling cooperation, fostering co-evolution, learning and innovation, and is committed to pluralism. In diversity it sees strength rather than division. Contemporary forms of virtual communication make the provision of transparent information easier, immediate and cheap. Whereas in the past the slow transmission of information, its necessary archiving and storing in written files, the high costs of reproduction, and limited literacy may all have conspired to make hierarchy more effective, because control was premised on institutionalized routines, that is no longer the case today. The conditions exist in which organizations can empower their members to be more responsibly autonomous, where members can be autonomous but responsible subjects with clear modes of accountability.

The emergence of virtual immediacy and instantaneity is driving hitherto hierarchical organizations to become increasingly either more heterarchical or responsibly autonomous, or both. Decisions can be made by secret ballot in virtual labs, where arguments for and against actions can be made anonymously on a shared screen. Here the power of good argument will prevail rather than the power of hierarchy, which presumes that enlightenment and wisdom reside in domination: a very dubious proposition (albeit one with a long historical pedigree emanating from the Age of Reason). In this shift, management ceases to direct and instead starts to facilitate organization processes for goal setting, standard setting and value-articulation. One corollary is that the cultural ties that bind will flourish and grow stronger in a climate of genuine responsibility and respect rather than in an inauthentic parroting of what are presumed, on the rule of anticipated reaction, to be views that will accord with those of people who are in positions of dominance.

Both heterarchy and responsible autonomy are specifications of different forms of rule by many (polyarchy), rather than rule by one, as in hierarchy.

Responsible autonomy means getting things done not through hierarchical control but through the autonomy of a group or individual to decide how they will do what they will do, where 'what they will do' means that they are accountable to some others; hence, the notion of responsible autonomy. Many organizational examples of low prescription/ high responsible autonomy come to mind, such as a research team or investment fund management, where, if a fund does well, the manager may be given more funds to invest and earn more accordingly from fees and commissions. Here, autonomy is provided by the internal policies of the financial institution where accountability is evident in the way that the fund performs in a competitive market. Fairtlough sees responsible autonomy as flourishing best where it is encapsulated within rules that are widely understood, transparent, legitimated and shared, and where action is open to critique, such as regular audit, or being held in some way accountable for the actions taken as a responsibly autonomous subject or unit. Many forms of audit are increasingly institutionalized to hold people accountable at a distance, such as the growth of standards. The essence of responsible autonomy is that there is audit and dispute determination by some independent and third party held in good standing, and institutionalized as such.

In heterarchy, as Fairtlough explains it, through rotation of office, and reward schemes related to risk and innovation rather than position, tendencies to domination can be reduced. Heterarchy builds democratic skills and capabilities in what has the potential to be a virtuous circle; it encourages more sophisticated general skills for interpersonal processes, dialogical relations, teamwork, mutual respect and openness. Admittedly, as Fairtlough suggests, heterarchies work best when the size of the organization is small: below about 150 people, he recommends. Heterarchy cannot be extended indefinitely as it is impossible to work in what are highly direct democracies once the number of participants rises beyond the circle of people who can know each other reasonably well.

What distinguishes heterarchy from responsible autonomy is that in the former there is a constant and continuous interaction between entities and agents in deciding what to do and how to do it. In many instances, this means that for heterarchy to be successful it needs to develop an identity separate from whatever organizational bodies comprise and host the constituent parts. Responsible autonomy means that there can be a lot more distance between agencies. Both differ from hierarchy in not being subject to arbitrary power vested only in relations of domination. No pure versions of these types will be found in reality; they are abstracted 'ideal' types, in the Weberian sense. Most organizations will comprise different mixes of hierarchy (or direct control), heterarchy and responsible autonomy. The benefits and costs of each will differ in different contexts.

The new edition of this book extends the argument of the first edition. It does so by drawing on the work of Michael Thompson in the field of cultural theory. Fairtlough introduces Michael Thompson as one of the most innovative thinkers in the social sciences and sets out the distinct 'ways of life' proposed by Thompson, four of which he termed fatalism, hierarchy, individualism and egalitarianism. Fairtlough takes these typologies of hierarchy, egalitarianism and individualism, lays them over his three ways of getting things done (hierarchy, heterarchy and responsible autonomy) and exposes an uncanny correspondence between them.

Having established a correspondence between the types, Fairtlough argues that the dynamic interaction between the elements derived from what he terms triarchy theory and from cultural theory can explain shifts and changes in organizations. Thus, as organizations cease to work or are put under pressure, people will respond by shifting positions between typologies and take the organizational model through a variety of possible group/grid movements.

Responsible autonomy reflects the pioneer, whilst heterarchy, with its creative compartments, offers an egalitarian, more democratic organization. However, a static position (more probable in hierarchy than in the other forms because it is high grid/high group) is likely to reduce the creativity and success of an organization.

Fairtlough also incorporates an examination of Roberto Unger's work on a wide range of European and Asiatic societies. Unger uses the concept of plasticity as a key way of understanding the economic and military success of these societies. Plasticity allows for variation in ways of getting things done, of which Fairtlough argues that there are only three. Unger de-emphasizes hierarchy and stresses the importance of experimenting with alternatives. This coincides with Fairtlough's own view – as does Unger's view of innovations.

Unger finds that plasticity increases with two factors: the first of these is a reduction in the distinction between the roles of task-definition and task-execution, which is roughly speaking the distinction between those who manage and those who do the work. Allied to this is a reduction in the distinctions between different work-roles, between those of the specialist and the generalist, between those of the expert and the enthusiast, between staff and line.

Fairtlough argues that a dedication to increasing plasticity in organizational arrangements, along with openness, mutual trust and skill in interpersonal process, are the key factors that promote heterarchy. The concept of plasticity addresses the underlying reasons for change and the skills required in making it happen.

Fairtlough's argument that cultural theory adds to triarchy theory is important, first, in that the probable correspondence between the theories helps to answer the question: why are there only three ways of getting things done? Second, it opens the way to build models that show the interaction between the three ways in which things might be done. The introduction of plasticity into the equation demonstrates how the dispersal of power and softening of roles creates the right conditions for successful change in organizations.

Fairtlough echoes a general view in seeing the development of knowledge-based organizations as major drivers of a shift away from hierarchy towards heterarchy and responsible autonomy. A knowledge economy's virtual communications replace the need for rules, precedents and files to record them, and greater knowledge means increased scrutiny, awareness and possibility of audit or whistle blowing. However, default settings have a way of becoming deeply sedimented, not only in Microsoft products or vehicle design, but in organization design more generally. In the past, organization design has been largely the preserve of the engineers: functionalists to the core. With Fairtlough, the combination of experiential artistry, wisdom, and deeply reflective practice positions a different kind of creative thinking at the forefront of organization design. We have nothing to lose but a history that has held us captive for too long.

Stewart Clegg

Professor, University of Technology, Sydney and Aston Business School

1   Introduction

1.1   The Hegemony of Hierarchy

Suppose that most of us, without knowing it, are addicted to hierarchy. Addiction to hierarchy might be like addiction to stress, which is stimulating and even exciting, but eventually drains our energy and spoils our lives. Or addiction to hierarchy might be like addiction to alcohol. Modest quantities, of good quality, are delightful, but excess is nasty. Drinkers who don't recognize when they are overdoing it get into serious trouble. For addicts, the first step in kicking the habit is to understand the addiction. If indeed we are unconscious hierarchy-addicts, then we ought to seek a deeper understanding of hierarchy's appeal.

Hegemony makes a situation seem normal to nearly everyone – taken for granted and never questioned. When nearly everyone finds hierarchy to be a normal and inevitable part of organization this leads to the hegemony of hierarchy.

How is it possible to be a hierarchy-addict without knowing it? It happens through the hegemony of hierarchy. The term 'hegemony' derives from the Greek word for ruler. However, its main use today follows that of Antonio Gramsci. He uses the term to describe an overall dominance that creates ways of seeing the world that are accepted as normal by nearly everyone. Hegemony exists when a situation is always taken for granted and is never questioned. I believe it is correct to say that nearly everyone finds hierarchy to be a normal and necessary part of organization. This automatic assumption that hierarchy is inevitable is a key part of its hegemony.

Talk about organization usually centres on who should be in charge. We're used to hierarchy and know how it works. It's a familiar and comfortable habit, the obvious fall back, the default option. When it works, it feels precise and clear – we know Bloggs is the boss, he tells us what to do. When it doesn't work, we blame Bloggs. We accept that hierarchy has its faults, but we think it's inevitable. We may try to ameliorate its bad effects, but we never question the basic idea.

There have been hierarchies throughout history and hierarchies exist today in every part of the world. Hierarchy really can be comfortable – it appeals to the 'child' in us and is easier than alternatives that demand an adult, independent stance. Senge and Wheatley describe hierarchy as a whipping boy: something to blame for an organization's ills while forgetting that we are the ones creating it, or at the very least tolerating it. Rosabeth Moss Kanter says that hierarchies depend on fear and comfort: fear of powerful figures at the top and comfort with familiar patterns of relationships. These are factors that support the hegemony of hierarchy.

Hierarchy may have genuine value in organizations, but we will only be able to make a balanced judgement about its usefulness when its hegemony stops and it is seen as just one among several options.

It is possible that hierarchy has genuine value in organizations, and perhaps in society in general. But we will only be able to make a balanced judgement about hierarchy's usefulness when its hegemony stops and it is seen as just one among several options. The aim of this short book is to look objectively at hierarchy. I want to show why it has such a grip on us. I want to discuss it as just one possible way for getting things done in organizations. I want to inhibit thinking about hierarchy as inevitable or as if it were sacred.

Actually, the word 'hierarchy' started out with a sacred meaning. A hierarch was originally a chief priest, and hierarchy was originally the power-structure of the angels – seraphim, dominations, archangels and the like. So the concept may still carry an aura of the sacred, even though today the term 'hierarchy' generally means 'single rule'. Thomas Hobbes argued that without a single sovereign to keep order, chaos would ensue, bringing a war of all against all. He was writing when the divine right of kings was strongly asserted and when the role of priests was to mediate between the sacred and common humanity. Hobbes was inspired in part by a fear of civil strife. But he also wrote to please the powerful, to reinforce the idea that power should be concentrated, not dispersed.

Today it is widely accepted that organizations have to keep on learning if they are to survive. If hierarchy, such an important aspect of organization, goes unquestioned, this surely inhibits learning, since to learn requires us to ask questions and to be open to new things. On the whole, organizations have a pretty poor reputation. We make huge efforts to improve our organizations, but they so easily slip back into to dysfunction. Perhaps the hegemony of hierarchy is to blame for this.

The hegemony of hierarchy makes us think the only alternative is disorganization and stops us giving serious thought to proper alternatives. We only compare hierarchy with anarchy or chaos.

Because its hegemony leads us to think that hierarchy is the natural way to organize, we often feel that the only alternative is disorganization. If this were so, then hierarchy would indeed be inevitable. But, in fact, there are two excellent alternatives – ones that don't lead to chaos. These two are called heterarchy and responsible autonomy. The names will be strange to most people. The strangeness isn't surprising. Because of our addiction to hierarchy we don't, and indeed can't, give serious thought to its alternatives. Whether hierarchy is desirable, or not, in a particular situation, we don't know, because it never gets tested against anything other than anarchy or chaos.

A cynic might say that, if everyone agrees about the inevitability of hierarchy, it will be impossible to change. Certainly it won't be easy. However, two hundred years ago aristocratic domination was considered inevitable. One hundred years ago so was patriarchal rule. Change away from these was strongly resisted, but it happened. It could be that hierarchy in organizations is a further idea whose end is nigh, driven by social, intellectual and technological change.

1.2   Why I Wrote this Book

In my youth I thought, just like everyone else, that hierarchy was a natural and necessary part of organizations. It took years for me to begin to doubt that this was so, and more years before I started to explore the alternatives to hierarchy. But in the end I have become convinced that it is vital to question hierarchy's inevitability and to develop alternatives

We must question the inevitability of hierarchy if our businesses are to become more profitable and creative, if our government agencies are to become more effective and if our non-governmental organizations are to make real changes in the world and act in a really responsible way.

to it. Tinkering isn't enough; huge shifts are needed if our businesses are to become more profitable and creative, if our government agencies are to become more effective, and if our non-governmental organizations are to make real changes in the world and act in a really responsible way.

I have spent over fifty years in and around organizations – working in junior and senior positions in existing organizations and playing a key role in founding several new ones. I have served on bodies such as university councils and national research councils, giving me further understanding of the way organizations work. Although I am not an academic, and although I was trained in the natural sciences, I have read widely in the fields of organization and innovation studies, and in the social sciences generally, and written a good many books and articles in these fields. The aim is to combine theory with experience to produce thoroughly practical insights and proposals about the future of organizations.

Hierarchy is found not only in organizations, but also in society in general and in non-organizational groupings, like the family. However, this book is primarily about organizations. This is for three reasons. First, because organizations are my area of expertise. Secondly, because organizations are the place where hierarchy is most strongly hegemonic. In the twenty-first century, democracy is accepted, sometimes hypocritically, sometimes genuinely, as the best way to govern countries. In the family, patriarchal hierarchy is under siege. It is only in organizations that the rule of hierarchy remains virtually unchallenged. Thirdly, because organizations are central to twenty-first century life. Human beings spend a great deal of their time in and around organizations – being educated in them, working for them, subject to control by them. Making organizations function better, and become better places to work, would be a big contribution to human happiness.

My method in this book is to expound some general principles and to develop some general models useful in all organizations. I also tell stories about organizations, real and imagined, which illustrate and enliven these principles and models. Mostly, my arguments are based on organizational learning, on efficiency and effectiveness, on success in achieving organizational purposes, including increased profits for business. But I do not neglect the possibility that alternatives to hierarchy are morally desirable, that they could help people lead better lives.

James Ogilvy, who gave us the idea of organizational heterarchy, is outstanding in his ability to draw on the discipline of philosophy to provide practical advice for organizations. He has written:

You have a past; you have experiences and core competencies. Know them, use them and don't forget them. [But] don't be bound by your past. Feel free to reinvent yourself and your [organization] for an uncertain future.

I hope this book will be the starting point for a wider debate on hierarchy and on alternative ways for getting things done in organizations. I hope the debate will appeal both to those who feel hierarchy is inevitable, but are willing to listen to a different view, and to those who already know that other approaches work, but need help in convincing their colleagues.

1.3   The Shape of the Book

In the section following this introduction, I describe **how hegemony works and how it translates into an addiction to hierarchy.** In Section 3, I explain **what organizations really need** in order to function well. In Section 4, I describe the **three ways of providing for these needs and for getting things done** in organizations. These three ways are hierarchy and its two alternatives of heterarchy and responsible autonomy. In the subsequent section, I set out the **advantages for each of the three ways.**

In Section 6, I look at **parallels between cultural theory and triarchy theory**, then in Section 7, I show that **in real-life organizations we always find blends of the three ways**. It is the proportion in the blend that differs from organization to organization. I explore which blends suit which circumstances. In Section 8, I describe the **personal skills and institutional arrangements** that support moves towards heterarchy and responsible autonomy in organizations.

In the final section, I discuss why it is likely that **the time is now ripe** for a move away from our automatic assumption that hierarchy is the best way to get things done. Mainly through examples, I show how we can start **changing the blend of the three ways**, so as to gain the advantages of reduced hierarchy.

The *Notes* section at the end of the book has references to sections in the text. It provides additional material on certain topics and references to the *Bibliography*. In these two sections, you can find the works I've drawn on in writing the book.

I have not thought it necessary to provide an index for this short work. However, there is a comprehensive list of contents and the *Glossary* defines key terms and gives references to the sections in the text where the key terms are discussed.

2   A Basis for Hegemony

2.1   *How Hegemony Works*

During the twentieth century the term 'hegemony' came to mean the dominance of one or other way of looking at the world, in which intellectual, political and cultural aspects are combined.

Hegemony results in a way of seeing that is accepted as normal, as common sense. Although this way of seeing favours the interests of a dominant class, hegemonic ideas have a momentum of their own, which has allowed them to be taken for granted for centuries. Thus, when communism took over in the Soviet Union, the hegemony of many old ideas persisted, including a continued acceptance of the inevitability of hierarchy in organizations.

There are many possible explanations for the persistence of hegemonic ideas, but I believe that genetic predisposition is a critical factor. For example, it is well established in biology that animals, including humans, act in ways that favour their relatives. The innate bias we have towards others who share the same genes might well make it easy for ideas like nationalism to develop their hegemonic power, through the extension of the concept of relatedness to cover a whole nation. And if there were to be human genetic predisposition towards hierarchy, that would make it natural for hierarchy to become hegemonic.

Hegemony becomes established when the interests of the powerful coincide with a widespread genetic predisposition. Once established, hegemony becomes self-perpetuating.

It seems reasonable, therefore, to suggest that hegemony becomes established when the interests of the powerful coincide with a widespread genetic predisposition. Furthermore, once established, hegemonic tradition becomes self-perpetuating. In the rest of this section, I explore the influence on the hegemony of hierarchy of genetic predisposition, of the interests of the powerful, and of tradition.

2.2 Genes

We all know that chickens have pecking orders. The dominant bird pecks all the others; the lowliest is pecked by everyone else. Of course, poultry behaviour is only crudely analogous to that of humans. Chimpanzees give us more subtle analogies. There is a hierarchy within each group, and this hierarchy is more marked among males than females. The top male chimpanzee is not necessarily the strongest; instead, he is usually the one best at manipulating social coalitions to his advantage.

Among humans, hierarchy spontaneously emerges in groups of all kinds. Incipient hierarchies can be

7

Rape, murder and race hate are probably 'in our genes' – but they can largely be stopped by the right social institutions.

seen in groups of preschool children and in gangs of adolescents. Culture, as well as genes, affects such groups, but the fact that the phenomenon is so cross-cultural strongly suggests a genetic influence. We can ask: if it's in our genes, isn't hierarchy inevitable? In reply, we can say: there are lots of other human behaviours with a genetic predisposition which we can nevertheless succeed in avoiding – alcohol and nicotine addiction, for instance. Behaviours like rape, murder and race hate are probably also 'in our genes', but fortunately legal and moral prohibitions against them often become effective, because the new benefits greatly outweigh the old.

The prowling rivals round an alpha male are willing to risk a beating on the off-chance of getting some sex with the alpha's females. The genes for sexual persistence are the ones with the best chance of getting passed on. As Matt Ridley says, it is not so much the survival of the fittest that counts, but the *reproduction* of the fittest. This is the biological basis for the drive to get to the top of a hierarchy. The males at the top are the ones who father children. And females' genes encourage this; they want sons with genes for successful reproduction. All kinds of human behaviour, like keeping up with the Joneses, interest in the antics of celebrities or wanting a fast car, can be traced back to those genes – genes that selfishly want to be reproduced. High status leads to sex and to resources that nurture the offspring who carry the genes.

But that isn't the whole story. Television shows us exciting clashes between the top male and his junior rivals, but the truth is that much of the time the juniors accept their position. If you get wiped out in a frontal attack on the top male, your genes will have no chance of being passed on. Patient, submissive behaviour may be a better bet. There must be genes that predispose towards submission as well as genes encouraging dominance.

Along with these tendencies towards dominance and submission, there is a further tendency: intense interest in hierarchical matters – who's up and who's down. The concept of hierarchy is pretty simple, but in practice its ramifications are complex, because usually many people are involved, all wishing to play the hierarchical game in different ways. When people have made a successful investment in understanding their local hierarchies and in adapting to them, they will want these hierarchies to continue. They are the ones who tell you that hierarchy is inevitable. So, the human genetic inheritance contains an urge to be top, an urge to submit and a fascination with hierarchy. These predispositions differ from person to person, not only between the sexes but within them too. But it seems reasonable to claim that most of us share these predispositions, and that they reinforce the hegemony of hierarchy.

The human genetic inheritance gives us an urge to be top, an urge to submit and a fascination with hierarchy.

2.3 Hierarchy in Organizations

Today, organizations have a pretty poor reputation. We make huge efforts to improve them, but they so easily slip back into dysfunction. Why is that? Perhaps we have missed something universal and fundamental. I think that over-dependence on hierarchy may be the problem. We should, therefore, examine carefully the role of hierarchy. The truth is that we don't have to resort automatically to hierarchy when we want to get things organized. There have been hierarchies throughout history and hierarchies exist today in every part of the world. Yes, the habit is strong. But there can be better ways of working together. These alternatives are not soft options. Rather, they require people to take on more responsibility and to produce hard-nosed results – better results than hierarchy. We need to kick the bad habit of automatically choosing hierarchical organization. We can do this through a better understanding of hierarchy and its alternatives.

We need to kick the bad habit of automatically choosing hierarchical organization. We can do this through a better understanding of hierarchy and its alternatives.

Many people have an image of themselves that depends on their hierarchical position. For instance, someone could build his life around mingling with the mighty, and name-dropping to the less mighty. If this is combined with a talent for flattery, such a

9

life might become materially pretty comfortable. The satirical journal 'Private Eye' has a column that each week awards the Order of Brown Nose (OBN) to a select few of those whose flatteries have recently appeared in print. Hierarchy is obviously important to candidates for this award.

Someone who revels in personal power and who likes to kick people around can build and project an image of himself as a no-nonsense achiever. Hierarchical position legitimizes such a self-image. Without hierarchy, the image might collapse, leaving the person feeling lost or worthless. For such a person, hierarchy isn't just a comfort, it's a necessary support.

2.4   The 'Great Man'

Another reason for the persistence of hegemony is belief in the 'great man'. When something goes wrong with the profits of a business, with the popularity of a political party or with the artistic standards of an orchestra, the first impulse usually is to look for a new CEO, a new leader or a new conductor. But Tolstoy wrote, "The life of nations cannot be summarized in the lives of a few men, for the connection between these men and the nations has not been discovered." He goes on to say that the theory that this connection is based on the transference of the collective will of a people to certain historical personages is a hypothesis not supported by the experience of history.

The theory persists nonetheless. For example, both the USA and Britain have appointed so-called Drugs Tsars to coordinate a fight against illegal drugs. Perhaps the hope is that by putting the right person in charge there will be effective action. Or perhaps the aim is only to look good – the grandiose name given to the post and the hype surrounding the appointment suggest this might be the case. Either way, the appointment shows a belief in hierarchy – whether an actual belief in the principle or a cynical use of voters' belief in it.

Of course, an energetic, intelligent, dedicated, charismatic and lucky person at the top of an organization can make a difference, especially as a catalyst for obviously necessary changes. But in reality, as Tolstoy tells us, every one of the people who take part in a war (or in growing a firm or in raising funds for victims of an earthquake) makes it happen. Every leader depends on willing and capable followers. We may be willing to follow a leader in whom we believe, but we make our own decision to do so.

Every leader depends on willing and capable followers. We may be willing to follow a leader in whom we believe, but we make our own decision to do so.

2.5 Tradition

There is a long tradition of support for hierarchy in political and social science. Thomas Hobbes argued that without a sovereign to keep order, there would be a war of all against all. Max Weber argued that whether or not an organization exists depends entirely on the presence of a person in authority, and that assured power to issue commands must always be provided for. For writers like these, and for their numerous followers, the absence of hierarchy means the absence of order, of discipline, of system, of motivation, of leadership.

If we take hierarchies for granted, hierarchy seems the only way for organizations to allocate tasks, make rules and develop culture. These are necessary and we assume that this makes hierarchy necessary too.

In any properly functioning organization, tasks must be divided, rules and systems must be established and culture must be maintained and developed. If we take hierarchies for granted, the only way we can envisage for task-division, rule-setting and culture-development is for the hierarchy to do it. We know these things are necessary and we assume that this makes hierarchy necessary too. We assume that the choice is between hierarchy and anarchy. But this is not so – there are successful alternatives.

I have worked for many years in both the petrochemical and pharmaceutical industries. In both, it is vital that everyone has a highly disciplined approach to their work. Many people will say that this proves the need for hierarchy – you can't have a bunch of hippies fooling around with hundreds of

11

You can't have a bunch of hippies running a plant full of explosive hydrocarbons. But would you rather have the plant operated by trained professionals, for whom pride in safe working is part of their personal identity, or by people who only work safely because they are afraid of the boss? The identification of discipline with hierarchy is a dangerous mistake.

tons of highly explosive hydrocarbons. But think about it. Would you rather have the plant operated by trained professionals, for whom pride in safe working is part of their personal identity, or by people who only work safely because they are afraid of the boss? The identification of discipline with hierarchy is a mistake – a dangerous mistake. Actually, it's the professionalism of the work force that matters.

In a strictly hierarchical organization, the only learning that takes place is the learning of the individual at the top. Everyone else obeys orders. An organization without learning will only survive in very stable conditions. In practice, of course, the lower ranks actually learn and adapt without being told to do so. But hierarchies tend to learn slowly, especially because a lot of effort goes into preserving the superior status of those at the top: inevitably an anti-learning activity.

Leadership is not the same as hierarchy. A charismatic leader can have influence without any kind of command structure – think of Nelson Mandela leading from prison. Practice today in a few organizations shows it is possible to have dispersed leadership, with everyone in an organization able to give a lead when needed.

When I present this pretty negative view of hierarchy, I normally provoke quite a bit of resistance. Some people reject the idea of hierarchy-related genetics. They may accept that the human brain is 'hard-wired' for certain tasks – for instance, language – but find hard-wiring for hierarchy unlikely. Others accept that genetic influence is important, but say that therefore we can do nothing to change our ways of organizing. Yet others believe that because many successful organizations are hierarchical, hierarchy must be good.

There is ample evidence that hierarchy is not necessary for discipline, for systematic ways of working, for inspiration or for leadership.

Nevertheless, I think there is ample evidence that hierarchy is not necessary for discipline, for systematic ways of working, for inspiration or for leadership. The alternative to hierarchy is not chaos

12

or anarchy. Only our powerful addiction to hierarchy, given to us by our genes and by our culture, leads us to believe this.

In practice, many hierarchies are largely symbolic, meaning that those who are supposed to be in charge may contribute nothing to the organization's actual task or mission. The top person may get praised or blamed, but actually he/she doesn't affect outcomes. In these organizations hierarchy is an epiphenomenon – the real day-to-day learning and functioning of such organizations is largely disconnected from the hierarchy.

3   What Organizations Need

3.1   Coordination of Ends and Means

To discuss objectively the place of hierarchy in organizations and what its alternatives are, we ought first to consider what organizations need in order to function effectively. (An 'effective' organization is one that is able to achieve its purposes or aims.)

Human beings can achieve some things by themselves, but to achieve many other things they have to work in cooperation with others – or, to put it another way, they have to coordinate their actions. **Whenever people cooperate over time and in order to get things done, there is an organization.** For example, in businesses, people coordinate their actions in order to supply goods and services, and to make money. In schools, teachers cooperate to educate the young. In armies, soldiers coordinate their actions in order to fight battles. In political parties, politicians cooperate so as to gain power. In NGOs, people cooperate with the hope of changing the world.

A group of people is not the same as an organization. For example, the members of the audience at a concert don't need to coordinate their actions, except to clap at the right time, and anyway their association is

13

only temporary. A social club, whose members meet regularly, is hardly an organization, at least if it has no further purpose than conviviality. The inhabitants of a village can live alongside each other sociably, without being an organization. However, if the village is to have an annual flower and produce show, they will need a small organization whose purpose is to make the show happen.

By 'getting things done', I mean carrying out certain tasks in order to achieve certain purposes.

The distinction between organizations (which have common purposes and coordinated actions and which endure for a reasonable period) and non-organizational groups (which lack purposes, coordinated action and duration) is a fuzzy one. Even so, it is usually clear what is an organization and what isn't. The purposes of an organization tend to change over time, often gradually and occasionally abruptly. Simply to survive is usually one objective; growth is often another. Whatever their purposes are, organizations have to carry out various tasks. So, we can say that organizations enable people to collaborate on tasks and to achieve shared goals. Both means and ends are coordinated. By 'getting things done', I mean carrying out certain tasks in order to achieve certain purposes.

Coordination of ends and means requires four features: system, culture, leadership and power.

Coordination of ends and means requires four features: system, culture, leadership and power. I will discuss each of these in turn.

3.2   System

Organizations get lots of advantages from having systematic procedures, routines and standard operating procedures. Proper systems avoid wasteful re-invention. They prevent sloppy practices like 'making it up as you go along'. And if everyone follows a set of carefully designed rules, serious mistakes can usually be avoided. When good systems have been established, people feel secure. A good example is the need for safety procedures that take account of unlikely, but dangerous, possibilities. Another example is fair procedures for the recruitment of staff.

14

'Enabling' systems are good; 'coercive' systems are bad.

Organizations with many established systems and standard operating procedures are often called 'bureaucratic'. This carries the implication that their systems are cumbersome or stifling. You are obliged to fill in a questionnaire of some kind; you aren't sure why it is required and how it might be used; you get no feedback – this is a common experience of a coercive system. Coercive systems are those imposed when Big Brother is watching you, hoping to catch you out, or when an elite gathers information for its exclusive use. But, in fact, systems and rules often make life easier, by preventing careless mistakes, regularly providing useful information or structuring communication. These are called 'enabling' systems. Enabling systems are highly desirable and are very different from 'coercive' systems.

Economical, robust and user-friendly systems aren't easy to develop, because they need lots of trials and consultations with users. However, once they are in place, these enabling systems appear natural and aren't burdensome. You could say a proper enabling system is light and strong.

3.3   Organizational Culture

Systems help to coordinate action; so does an organization's common culture. A shared culture makes for good communication because words and phrases are less likely to be misunderstood. For instance, people will think more or less the same about the role of a project team or about the importance of a performance review. Within a common culture, people will have similar mental models of how things work. These could be the models people have of natural processes, of the working of machinery, of interpersonal dynamics, of academic disciplines, of economics or of politics.

In a common culture, people will tell the same stories, believe the same myths, share a lot of gossip, sing the same songs, be familiar with the same images and symbols. They will share many values, meaning that their ideas of right and wrong, or success and failure, will be much the same, at least as far as organizational matters are concerned. Mostly, a common culture emerges from the daily interaction of participants in the organization. They learn a culture just by being part of it. But a certain amount of culture-building can be deliberate – through ritual and ceremony, speeches and celebration.

Sometimes members are aware of their organization's cultural characteristics, sometimes they aren't. Sometimes cultural understanding is wholly tacit, sometimes partly explicit. Cultures are sometimes open and trusting, sometimes furtive and suspicious. But whatever it is like, a culture has a big influence on the way people work together in an organization.

Like its systems, an organization's culture can be either enabling or coercive, or some combination of the two.

Just like its systems, an organization's culture can be either enabling or coercive, or some combination of the two. At one extreme, there is an ambiance of fear, favouritism, malicious gossip and dishonesty. At the other extreme, there is frankness, mutual respect, shared commitment to goals, loyalty and fun.

3.4 Leadership

Leadership involves sense-making, vision and persuasion.

A leader is someone who can make sense of what is happening in and around the organization and can help others do the same. A leader has the vision to see what should be done and can persuade others to follow. So leadership involves sense-making, vision and persuasion.

A common picture of a leader is of a charismatic, egocentric individual who tells others what to do. But leadership doesn't have to be like that. Jim Collins says that the best leaders combine personal humility with professional will. When a leader has humility, there is less danger that his or her ego will be served rather than the organization.

Leadership is needed to define an organization's purposes, and to make sure these purposes are understood and agreed by people in the organization.

At times, purposes will have to evolve and leadership will then be necessary in proposing and negotiating changes. The tasks needed to achieve the organization's aims must be defined and people have to understand the tasks properly and become committed to carrying them out. For all this, leadership is vital.

In an organization, anyone who has an ethos of service can be a leader.

In principle, anyone in an organization can be a leader: anyone who has an ethos of service to the organization and to its stakeholders. Leaders do not have to be officially appointed. Anyone committed to sustaining or developing the organization's purposes can exercise leadership, sometimes only occasionally – for instance when the person concerned feels particularly strongly about an issue, or has special expertise. When everyone has the opportunity to be a leader, and a good many people actually show leadership, this is called 'dispersed leadership'.

3.5   Power

Power is necessary for getting things done, but often it is concealed.

Power is a necessary part of getting things done. In the majority of organizations today, power is concealed. The reasons for this are that a display of power may provoke resistance and concealed power is less likely to be questioned. There are exceptions. In a mafia, for instance, power is kept on display, because the capo wants to be seen by his followers and his rivals as capable of anything.

The ultimate source of power may be violence, as in the mafia example. Violence is also a key part of the power of the state, which always has the police and the army in the background. States seek a monopoly of violence in their territories.

Power also comes from control of resources, particularly money. This happens most forcefully in cases when starvation is the alternative to doing what a rich person wants. Although that is an extreme case, those who have their own money, or control the use of an organization's resources, have power to get others to do what they want.

Power may have quite a mild form in many organizations. Power can be legitimate – for instance when elected politicians act with the consent of the governed. Then a different name may be used – power may be called 'authority'. The power of the better argument, and power derived from experience or expertise, are also legitimate – and in these cases power may be called 'influence'. The charisma of the power-holder may be important, too.

Power can operate in impersonal ways. Rules and routines, once they become habitual, can exercise control. Similarly, when belief systems and ideologies are internalized they become controlling. The human need to belong, for membership and identity, can be a source of power. Of course, behind impersonal power are actual people. Somewhere, individuals are making the rules, doing the indoctrination, organizing the discipline or granting membership. There does not have to be a single person or a small group pulling the strings, with the rest of us being the puppets. Power often arises from the dispersed actions of many people. Even so, it is important to remember that actual people are involved and that all of them have some power, even if the distribution of power is uneven – which it is in most organizations.

Power is in constant flux; it is dynamic; its use always provokes resistance.

Power is frequently thought of as if it were a thing – a magic wand or a Field Marshal's baton. Stewart Clegg shows that a more accurate view of power is that it is in constant flux, that it is dynamic. On this view, if power is not used, it withers. Its use always provokes resistance of some kind, resulting in an interaction between opposing power-plays. This dynamic view of power sees it as a matter of shifting alliances and stratagems, of contestation and struggle. For example, even if people in an organization obey its rules most of the time, situations will arise in which the rules aren't clear and need interpretation. Power may then become subject to open contest, making clear its dynamic character.

The title of Cynthia Hardy and Stewart Clegg's essay 'Some Dare Call It Power' implies that in most discourse about organizations, talk about power is suppressed. They write:

One consequence of the widespread, if implicit, acceptance of the hierarchical nature of power has been that social scientists have rarely felt it necessary to explain why it is that power should be hierarchical.

According to Hardy and Clegg, most writers on organizations choose to treat hierarchy as natural or legitimate. They do this, consciously or unconsciously, in deference to the hegemony of hierarchy. There are two important consequences. First, the taken-for-grantedness of hierarchy is reinforced. Secondly, the connection between power and hierarchy goes unexamined. Power is dismissed as either corrupt, when office-holders abuse their positions, or as rebellious, when the wishes of the hierarchy are challenged from below. As Hardy and Clegg put it, only 'bad guys' use power, the 'good guys' use something else – although the literature is not clear on exactly what.

Power is used both to reinforce the hegemony of hierarchy and to achieve organizational aims – but the two uses combine, blurring the nature of power.

Power is therefore used both to reinforce the hegemony of hierarchy and to achieve organizational aims. Nearly always, these two uses of power are closely intertwined, making it hard to understand the nature of power in organizations. Understanding hierarchy, by revealing its hegemonic grip, will make it easier to understand the operation of power, both in general and as it is exercised in a particular organization.

Struggle within an organization is inevitable, since individual aims are never fully aligned with those of the organization, and as diverse views of the world will lead to different opinions on how to get things done. Diversity in views is highly desirable, providing differences can be resolved constructively. Hierarchical resolution of disputes is what we're familiar with. It can provide a quick fix for a problem, perhaps at the cost of built-up resentment. Better means may be available, but they will require the use of power of some kind – including the power of the better argument.

3.6 'Exit' and 'Voice'

In addition to the four organizational needs – system, culture, leadership and power – which I've just discussed, there are a pair of further factors that must be borne in mind. Albert Hirschman points to two universal and complementary mechanisms that push failing organizations towards improvement, whether they are firms that fail to satisfy their customers, political parties whose policies are no longer attractive, or organizations of any kind that are not liked by their staff. Customers, party supporters or staff can respond in either or both of two ways, which Hirschman calls 'exit' and 'voice'.

'Exit' is when customers stop buying, supporters stop voting for the party's candidates, or staff resign. 'Voice' is when these groups make their views known to the organization, in the hope that their complaints will be heard and acted on. Traditional managements see exit as treason and voice as mutiny and may try to ignore both. But sooner or later they have to take note, at least if there are alternative organizations around for the dissatisfied to turn to.

3.7 Conclusion

Organizations need enabling systems, trust-generating cultures, serving leadership and accountable power. 'Exit' and 'voice' push organizations towards these.

Organizations cannot do without any one of the four features I've described: system, culture, leadership and power. All four strongly influence each other. Although all four are necessary, all of them can unfortunately work in ways that make the organization less effective in achieving its purposes. The ways in which the four features are used, therefore, need to be considered carefully. In order to be effective, an organization should have systems that are enabling rather than coercive; culture that is trustful not toxic; leadership that serves the whole organization rather than just the interests of leaders; and power that is accountable rather than domineering or manipulative. 'Exit' and 'voice' push organizations in these desirable directions.

Hierarchy has been the most commonly used way of combining system, culture, leadership and power in order to get things done. Because it is so common, it is often thought of as the only way. But there are other ways, and in the next section I explore these.

4   The Three Ways of Getting Things Done

4.1   Hierarchy

There are three, and only three, fundamental ways of getting things done: hierarchy, heterarchy and responsible autonomy.

I believe that in organizations there are three, and only three, fundamental ways of getting things done: hierarchy, heterarchy and responsible autonomy.

Hierarchy starts with a single supreme ruler at the top, whose will is supposed to control the whole of an organization. The supreme ruler passes authority on to a series of lesser rulers, and so on down the pyramid of the organization. Because it starts with a single ruler we can call hierarchy 'single rule'.

Hierarchy starts with a single supreme ruler, who passes authority on to a series of lesser rulers.

Monotheistic religions support the idea of a single ruler – Thou shalt have none other God but me. Authoritarian politics also emphasizes a single leader – One Country, one People, one Leader. The patriarchal family has a single Head of the Family. As noted earlier, the very idea of hierarchy has a sacred origin.

In organizations, the idea of single rule retains its power. Much of the time, Max Weber's writings are open-minded and exploratory. When it comes to the need for a hierarchy, however, he becomes dogmatic, stating categorically that whether or not an organization (a corporate group) exists depends entirely on the presence of a person in authority and on the presence of persons who can be counted on to carry out the orders of the one in authority.

But in religion, politics and the family, the idea of single rule has usually been qualified. Greece and Rome had pantheons of gods, most of whose members acted pretty independently. Milton's Satan was a rebel angel. Christianity has a Trinity. In Latin America, dictatorship often meant a Junta. Businesses have boards of directors. Even in the traditional family, mother was often the Chief Operating Officer.

4.2 Heterarchy

Heterarchy is multiple rule, a balance of powers rather than the single rule of hierarchy.

Heterarchy means 'multiple rule', a balance of powers rather than the single rule of hierarchy. It is a much less familiar term than hierarchy, although the general idea of shared rule has actually been around for a very long time. James Ogilvy introduced the term 'heterarchy' into the study of organizations.

Here are several examples of heterarchy:

- The first example is a trivial one: the children's game of rock, scissors and paper. In this game rock blunts scissors, scissors cut paper, paper wraps rock. None of the three is dominant. The relation between them is heterarchical.

- Partnerships, like those in law or accountancy firms, are partly heterarchical. At least in small firms, all partners are of roughly equal status, although they may elect a managing partner, thereby introducing an element of hierarchy. There is also hierarchy in the relation between the partners and the other people working in the firm – non-partner lawyers and support staff. Nevertheless, the key decisions remain heterarchical. A partner who wants to do something novel must convince his or her peers that the proposal will be good for the firm.

- Heterarchical relations are possible between units within organizations. Units like finance and human resources have authority over the way other units operate, at least for specific matters. For example, a human resources department can insist that recruitment of staff is carried out in a certain way. But the HR department is accountable to other departments for the effectiveness of the services it provides to them. This can be regarded as a separation of powers between the staff and line functions of the organization. Both HR and an operating department could ultimately be responsible to a common boss, and it could then be argued that this is an example of hierarchy, not heterarchy. But that doesn't alter the fact that the *relationship* between HR and the operating department is heterarchical.

- Strategic alliances between businesses are now quite usual. For instance, when a small biotechnology company discovers a promising drug, but does not have the resources for later-stage development and marketing, it usually seeks a partnership with a major pharmaceutical company. The relationship between the businesses is heterarchical, since each exerts an influence on the other and, at least in theory, neither party dominates the other.

- Heterarchy is the concept behind the *trias politicas* (or separation of powers) of political theory, for instance the separation of legislative, executive and judicial powers in the constitution of the United States.

- Although, in the geopolitical sphere, some states are more powerful, militarily or economically, than other states, there is a degree of mutual control between them – in other words, they have a heterarchical interrelation. Diplomacy is a practice used to manage this interrelation.

4.3 Responsible Autonomy

With responsible autonomy, a group decides what to do, but is accountable for the outcome. Accountability is what makes responsible autonomy different from anarchy.

The third way of getting things done is responsible autonomy. In this way, an individual or a group has autonomy to decide what to do, but is accountable for the outcome of the decision. It might be called 'no rule', or rather, no *external* rule. The existence of accountability distinguishes responsible autonomy from anarchy. Autonomy requires clearly defined boundaries at which external direction stops. Here are some examples:

- Adam Smith described the operation of autonomy in the economic sphere, where the actions of autonomous firms combine to generate the 'invisible hand' of the market. The need to generate enough cash to survive provides the necessary accountability. Financially successful firms survive and grow; unsuccessful ones do not. The invention of limited liability as a form of legal incorporation provided an important boundary between a company and its shareholders.

- Basic scientific research, in academe and in research institutes, is largely conducted by autonomous groups, which are led by principal investigators. These groups develop their reputations by publishing reports in peer-reviewed journals. Principal investigators apply for research grants from various funding bodies. Grants are given subject to the novelty and significance of the grant application and the reputation of the group. The principal investigator's freedom to choose research topics and to recruit people provides autonomy. The group's continued existence depends on its continuing to publish good science – this provides accountability.

- Investment management institutions usually give individual fund managers a lot of autonomy. If a fund does well, relative to the sector or to the market as a whole, its manager may be given a larger fund and will attract more clients. Autonomy is provided by the internal policies of the investment institution. Accountability is provided by the performance of the fund.

4.4   Complex Evolving Systems

The three examples I've just given not only illustrate the concept of responsible autonomy, but are also instances of Complex Evolving Systems. CES is a term used in the new field of complexity thinking to describe a system that is able to adapt and evolve and to create new order and coherence. The order created comes from the internal operation of the system, not from any external design or control. A CES is therefore an example of self-organization.

Complex Evolving Systems can include human beings, as, for instance, in the market example, but they can also be non-human. A prime example of a mainly non-human CES is Darwinian evolution, where the operation of natural selection enables organisms to evolve over time. Even a non-living CES is possible, for example a computer programme that evolves fantastic structures by following a few simple rules. A key feature of a CES is the emergence of order, sometimes intricate and innovative order, as a result of the operation of relatively simple principles.

To take a further example, in natural ecosystems, there is interaction between predators and their prey, between the elements of a food chain, or between generalist organisms, which range widely, and specialist ones, which find their own niches to exploit. From a huge variety of interactions, as time goes by, identifiable patterns emerge in the ecosystem and order appears from randomness.

Complex Evolving Systems exhibit self-organization, emergent properties and the generation of new order.

Thus Complex Evolving Systems are natural or human systems which exhibit self-organization, emergent properties and the generation of new order.

Within organizations, a group of sub-units with responsible autonomy can form a CES, generating

25

novelty and selecting the most useful of the novel ideas. Constantly improving performance is the result, given the right performance criteria against which selection is made. Internal markets are one form of organizational CES, but not the only one – there doesn't have to be trading between sub-units. If autonomous sub-units are rewarded for innovative ideas or for successful development of human talent, then a CES may result.

4.5   Encapsulation

The term 'encapsulation' is used by Amitai Etzioni to describe the process that creates market systems within societies. The process involves the formulation of rules, customary or legal, tacit or explicit, that govern the operation of markets. If nearly all participants in a market abide by the rules, then the market can function as a Complex Evolutionary System – or, as Adam Smith called it, a hidden hand. Within the rules, traders are free to operate as they like, and by working to benefit themselves, they generally benefit society as a whole. Encapsulation in society is much more than written rules. It is a subtle process, involving systems, learning, culture, communication and power. A capsule is the glove that Adam Smith's invisible hand must always have, whether or not we realize it.

In organizations, encapsulation requires: a commitment to stick by the rules; trust; clear boundaries and openness.

The concept also applies to autonomous elements within organizations. Within organizations, the process of encapsulation ought to be simpler than in society generally, but it still has to be a careful one, otherwise the benefits will not appear. What is needed is: first, everyone's commitment to sticking by the rules and widespread trust that others will almost always stick by them; secondly, clear boundaries for every capsule; and, thirdly, openness that enables all concerned to verify that rules are being followed, although others' tactics and strategies can remain secret.

4.6   Critique

Critique is what makes autonomy responsible and accountable.

Critique is a another term relating to responsible autonomy. Setting up critique can be regarded as a part of the process of encapsulation, because its rules must be clear from the start. It describes the process of evaluation, by external agencies, of the results of an autonomous unit. Indeed, it is what makes autonomy responsible and accountable. A good example of critique is the process of auditing and periodic reporting by limited liability companies, especially those whose shares are traded on a stock exchange. In this case, the process is backed by company law, by the listing requirements of stock exchanges, and by professional standards for audit.

Analysis by professionals in financial services firms, by credit-rating agencies, by journalists and by investors adds to critique and is based partly on companies' published figures and partly on other research. Companies try to influence the results of critique to make them as favourable as they can and sometimes they cheat, but, by and large, the process is reliable.

Critique can be directed towards matters that are not directly financial – for example the social and environmental performance of companies. Over the past two decades, specialist organizations devoted to this kind of critique have been set up and standards have been devised against which performance can be measured. Critique can be applied to organizations other than businesses. For example, league tables for schools and universities and appraisals of NGOs are now published regularly, as are certifications of foods as organic and toys as safe.

Organizations use critique to review the performance of their sub-units. If it is to support responsible autonomy, critique must be both firm and fair.

Organizations use critique to review the performance of their sub-units. If it is to support responsible autonomy, critique must be both firm and fair. External models, like those that form part of company law or of inter-organization comparison, can be used when internal mechanisms for critique are being devised.

4.7   Resolving Disputes

There are many reliable, non-hierarchical ways to resolve disputes.

Responsible autonomy will sometimes lead to disputes, for instance about the fairness of critique or interference in matters that are supposed to be within the capsule of an autonomous unit. There are external models for dispute resolution, like the law courts, arbitration procedures and the ombudsman system. At present, organizations generally use hierarchical methods to resolve disputes – the boss steps in and settles the matter. But it is perfectly possible to work out independent, heterarchical means of arbitration or judgement by third parties within the organization. Reliable methods for resolving disputes are part of effective encapsulation.

4.8   Heterarchy Compared with Responsible Autonomy

Heterarchy and responsible autonomy are non-hierarchical, but otherwise they are quite different.

These two ways of getting things done are similar in being non-hierarchical, but in other respects they are quite different. Heterarchy involves continuous interactions between individuals and sub-units in an organization as they decide what to do and how to coordinate their actions. The sheer density of this communication might require a lot of time and effort – a possible disadvantage for heterarchy. Responsible autonomy, if set up properly, means that sub-units are much more self-sufficient and that interaction between them is much less intense.

4.9   Ideal Types

Each one of the three ways of getting things done is what sociologists call 'an ideal type'. This means the concept is not encountered in its pure form in real organizations. For instance, no hierarchy, however dominant, can control everything. Likewise, because boundaries cannot, in practice, be drawn in a totally clear way, complete autonomy is never possible. And elements of hierarchy or autonomy will always creep into a heterarchical organization. So every actual

Every organization is a mixture of hierarchy, heterarchy and autonomy – in widely varying proportions.

organization is a mixture of hierarchy, heterarchy and autonomy – but in widely varying proportions.

All the same, the three concepts are valuable for gaining an understanding and discussing the different ways of getting things done in organizations. A full understanding of the three ways, and how they can be blended, will enable great improvements in organizations.

4.10 Are There Only Three Ways?

I am frequently asked why there are only three ways of getting things done in organizations. Well, I am not able to prove there are no further ways, but no one has been able to show me another. Various suggestions can be made. For instance, an organization might get things done through the love and respect that its members have for each other. But I don't think love and respect are sufficient as ways of getting things done. They can, of course, have a profound influence on the culture of an organization, but in themselves they do not provide system or leadership.

If my claim that there are three, and only three, ways to coordinate an organization is correct, then we can coin a name for the threesome: triarchy. The theoretical and practical study of how the three ways work, separately and together, could then be called triarchics.

4.11 The University of Barchester

To illustrate how hierarchy, heterarchy and autonomy can work in practice, I will tell the story of a fictitious organization called the University of Barchester. Although a fiction, from my experience with universities I believe the story to be pretty realistic.

Since its foundation in 1960 in a provincial English city, Barchester has out-paced most of its peer group, largely through the leadership of its Vice-Chancellor, Simon Goode, who was in post for the unusually long period of 17 years. Immediately he was appointed, Goode decided to build a small number of world-class Schools in the university. The way to achieve this was by getting a limited number of Schools into virtuous circles, in which initial excellence and excitement attracted good staff, good students and better funding, which generated even greater excellence, and so on.

This meant that weaker Schools would have to be closed. Of course this was not popular with these Schools, and Goode was accused of brutal managerialism and of perverting the whole idea of the university as a place for disinterested scholarship and research. Nevertheless, Goode persisted. When the School of Biology found it had three Fellows of the Royal Society on its staff, his policy began to be generally accepted. By the year 2000, the number of schools had been reduced to twelve. Of these, five schools were clearly recognized as internationally outstanding.

Of the other seven schools, six were top class by UK standards. The Law School was the only one that was less satisfactory. Goode's policy was to leave most of Barchester's schools to manage their own affairs, except when they were not performing. When this was so, he took great trouble to persuade academic staff that action was needed. Eventually, when the Senate considered his proposal to close the Law School, 80% voted in favour.

By the year 2000, this way of managing the university had done what it was intended to do and was welcomed by the majority of faculty members. Goode would be retiring in 2004. So far, he had himself done most of the university's strategic thinking. He felt that before he left there must be in place a more collective means for strategy-formation. He saw this taking the form of an annual planning cycle. Each autumn, a few small working groups would look carefully at Barchester's successes and failures, at student expectations and at intellectual trends. These working groups gave seminars on their conclusions that were open to all faculty members.

Early in the New Year, each school produced its five-year plan, which was reviewed with the Vice-Chancellor and then sent to all other schools. In March, a Strategy Day was held, attended by the VC and the Deans of all schools. The only formal output from this day was a list of strategic uncertainties, with dates by which they should be resolved, and a list of important future decisions, with dates by which they should be taken. Goode encouraged strategic conversation everywhere in the university, around the key uncertainties and key decisions. The purpose of these conversations was to be well prepared for each decision.

There was a risk that once Goode was gone, things would go wrong. One possibility would be to replace him with another 'strong' Vice-Chancellor, but this might be risky. He himself was a pretty forceful personality, but people had known him for years and had got used to his ways. It could be different for a newcomer who tried to dominate the place, perhaps provoking years of bitter conflict. Most Deans of Schools and many professors had become internationally well-known and could easily be lured away by other universities. Goode decided that it would be safer to replace his own role as the university's strategist by collective guidance. Deans would have to become less focused on their own needs and more focused on the university as a whole. It would, Goode thought, be best to get them to take collective responsibility for Barchester's future.

In this example, we can see the operation of all three ways for getting things done. The hierarchical role of Simon Goode was the main way in the early years. He had a vision of how Barchester could thrive in the situation in which British universities found themselves during the 1980s and 1990s. He had the personality, intellect and political savvy to convince the majority of his colleagues to follow that vision. He wasn't a bully, and he wanted colleagues as strong and clever as himself, but in those days he was definitely the boss.

31

As the Schools and their Deans grew in achievement and confidence, they became increasingly autonomous. Goode made sure that the budgeting and accounting systems of the university were adapted so that Schools could largely run their own affairs. When a School's quality of work attracted to the University increased funds for teaching and research from external sources, almost all of the extra money was passed on to the School. If a School wanted better lecture rooms, it could have them, but had to pay for them from its reserves. Continuing success in teaching and research and prudent management of its finances guaranteed continuing autonomy for a School.

By 2003, Goode had greatly reduced his hierarchical interventions. The Schools had become highly autonomous. The new strategic system was starting to work, making most faculty members feel they could have a genuine part in shaping Barchester's future. Anyone willing to contribute time and to think hard could influence the university's strategic conversation. Not everyone wanted to do this, of course, but they knew that they had the opportunity. Formal votes in Senate remained the final point of decision, but key decisions were only taken after widespread and serious debate. This was a heterarchical process. Each School naturally had an agenda of its own, but most Deans knew if they pushed too hard they would run into opposition. They might end up with less than they could get by a collegiate approach.

In any case, many decisions were taken heterarchically, without the involvement of the Senate. For a minor matter like the opening hours for a particular building, two or three Schools would negotiate a deal between themselves and inform the rest of the university. Simon Goode encouraged this kind of thing and helped it to develop by keeping central administration very small.

Certain central functions, like internal audit or health and safety, were strongly supported by him and had the resources they needed to do their work. Top quality external advice was also available, for instance for architectural design. But for many matters there was no central staff and, when needed, coordination was achieved by *ad hoc* working parties made up of people from the Schools. The central administration simply recorded and published the agreement made by a working party.

When Goode retired, the new Vice-Chancellor was recruited with the specific understanding that she was taking over a largely non-hierarchical organization, with autonomous Schools and mostly heterarchical decision-making. She responded by concentrating her personal time and effort on attracting the very best staff and students to the University, on acting as a facilitator and mentor to her colleagues, and on being an external advocate for the university. She exercised serving leadership and she made sure the central administration was an enabling bureaucracy.

In summary, the university moved from largely hierarchical, single rule towards a mix that was mainly heterarchical and autonomous. All three triarchic ways were involved, but the balance between them changed. That worked because the rules were well-understood, well-accepted and generally followed.

5   Advantages of Each of the Three Ways

5.1 *Advantages of Hierarchy*

Familiarity is the foremost advantage of hierarchy. Everyone has had long experience from childhood onwards of this way of getting things done. Familiar ways are reassuring ways. Hierarchy feels natural, we take it for granted, we have a deep understanding of it and it needs little explanation. Hierarchy not only feels natural, but it actually is natural – in the sense that humans have an inbuilt tendency towards it.

Familiarity and naturalness are undeniable and important advantages of hierarchy.

Familiarity and naturalness are undeniable and important advantages of hierarchy. However, making a conscious choice in favour of hierarchy (possibly because of these advantages) is a different matter from blindly accepting its inevitability.

Ever since Thomas Hobbes first made it in the seventeenth century, a claim that has been widely accepted is that hierarchy avoids the war of all against all. Hobbes was rightly concerned about the dangers of civil war and thought that the only way to avoid the dangers was to have a single powerful ruler who would stop all in-fighting. This claim was, of course, made in a political context, but it has been widely applied in organizational contexts. Put simply, the claim is that hierarchy prevents chaos.

The next advantage is that hierarchy goes beyond the simple avoidance of chaos and actually produces discipline and order. It is claimed that only with hierarchy can we get the benefits that come from well-trained people, who meticulously stick to laid-down procedures. We want tasks like aircraft maintenance to be done in a strict, unadventurous, disciplined manner and believe this can only be achieved through hierarchy. Max Weber was an influential proponent of this claim.

Leadership is also an advantage claimed to be available only through hierarchy. Experience of effective leadership from the appointed head of an organization, like Simon Goode's at the University of Barchester, is extended to mean that leadership can only come from the top.

In feudal times, hierarchy was thought to be the right way because those at the top were the only ones who knew how to get things done. The supreme ruler, the king, was born to rule. So were the lesser hierarchs, the aristocracy. The peasants were born to do as they were told. By the nineteenth century, this theory of superior birth had been replaced by a theory of superior education. Only the few with proper schooling, higher education or professional training were fit to make vital decisions. The equivalent theory today is that the most talented should have the top jobs, hierarchy being seen as the best means of using scarce talents.

A further advantage claimed for hierarchy is motivation. Climbing the ladder gives people something to strive for. Although only a few can get to the top, everyone makes great efforts to get there, because of the big rewards.

The final advantage of hierarchy is clarity or certainty. In some ways this is a summation of the other advantages. At least with hierarchy you know where you are. You know who makes the decisions. Even if you have a vacillating leader, you know who is producing the vacillations. When things go wrong everyone knows who is to blame. And there is also clarity about who you are. You know your present rank, with its responsibilities, and you know the future rank you hope to reach. Thus, hierarchy helps to define personal identity.

Familiarity, naturalness, prevention of chaos, discipline, leadership, use of scarce talent, personal motivation, personal identity and clarity are all claimed as advantages of hierarchy.

Familiarity, naturalness, prevention of chaos, discipline, leadership, use of scarce talent, personal motivation, personal identity and clarity; this is a formidable list of advantages for hierarchy. However, let us see what advantages there are for the other ways of getting things done.

5.2   Advantages of Heterarchy

Having thrown off rule from a distant sovereign in England, the Founding Fathers of the USA wanted to preclude the emergence of a home-grown tyrant. They therefore worked out a series of checks and balances, distributing political power between the President, the two houses of Congress and the judicial system and also between the Federal government and the governments of the states. They had had enough of the unchecked single rule of hierarchy. They replaced it with a large dose of heterarchy, although they did not use that term. This illustrates the first advantage

Heterarchy makes rulers more accountable and tyranny less likely.

of heterarchy: it makes rulers more accountable and tyranny less likely.

This is an example from the political sphere, where it is widely accepted that democracy is the best form of government. However, in the sphere of organizations, democracy is not at all accepted as the norm. After all, organizations do not have the same ultimate power as states: power that is backed by armies, police and prisons. Of course, there are some big corporate tyrants and lots of petty office tyrants, but is a heterarchical separation of powers really needed to deal with them?

It could be argued that employees, customers and shareholders of businesses can use the laws of the land to protect themselves. Employees can switch to other jobs, customers to other suppliers and shareholders into other investments. All of them have the 'exit' option. Furthermore, associations such as trades unions or consumer activist groups are there to help. Users of public services also have associations to put pressure on schools and hospitals and today there is usually an ombudsman to investigate apparent failures in tax or benefit systems and other administrative matters.

Legal redress, trades union support or ombudsman investigations are heterarchical resources available from outside the organization. It is good they are there. However, in many cases it would be far simpler and quicker if there were resources within the organization to deal with problems arising from the arbitrary use of power. Some large organizations do indeed have internal systems to which employees, customers and service users can appeal, but these systems often lack a reputation for being fair, effective and free from hierarchical dominance. Better internal systems might reduce the need for external ones. But either way, it is clear that heterarchy has a major advantage in that it provides accountability and reduces unchecked power. In organizations with good intentions, for example NGOs and charities, there can be a wish for heterarchy, because it feels morally better. But unless there is also a good understanding of human beings' tendency towards hierarchy and of the need for more than good intentions when getting things done, heterarchy can become simply a façade, behind which a hidden hierarchy runs the show. Skills and mechanisms that support heterarchy are discussed in Section 8 of this book. They are needed to prevent heterarchy degenerating into a façade, or an epiphenomenon.

Heterarchy entails more personal responsibility than hierarchy. Everyone is partly responsible for the whole, and everyone must have a reasonable knowledge of, and commitment to, the organization's vision and values.

5.3   The Evolution of Cooperation

In his famous book 'The Evolution of Cooperation', Robert Axelrod shows how cooperation spontaneously evolves between groups of people. He starts the book by asking:

Under what conditions will cooperation emerge in a world of egoists without central authority? This question has intrigued people for a long time. And for good reason. We all know that people are not angels, and that they tend to look after themselves and their own first. Yet we also know that cooperation does occur and that our civilization is based upon it. But in situations where each individual has an incentive to be selfish, how can cooperation ever develop?

In his book, Axelrod reports on computer simulations and real-life examples of cooperative behaviour. His conclusion is:

*We are used to thinking about competitions in which there is only one winner, competitions such as football or chess. But the world is rarely like that. In a vast range of situations mutual cooperation can be better for **both** sides than mutual defection. The key to doing well lies not in overcoming others, but in eliciting their cooperation [Original emphasis].*

37

The cooperation Axelrod describes depends on heterarchical interactions, showing that it is possible to do without the single, all-powerful ruler that Hobbes believed necessary if people were to cooperate. Solutions to conflicts and misunderstandings emerge by the modification of the behaviours of the parties concerned, leading to cooperation to mutual benefit. Although such self-generated solutions may take longer to emerge than an imposed solution, they tend to be more robust and more inventive.

5.4 Co-evolution

Complexity thinking has given us the concept of co-evolution. Two or more entities interact over time, each adapting itself to the behaviour of the other or others. All of the entities change through this co-evolutionary process. Contrast co-evolution with adaptation – for example an organization adapting to its environment. The organization is seen to change but the environment doesn't. Adaptation is one way only. Co-evolution is different. Co-evolution happens in a network of elements, all of which change as they interact and thereby influence each other. The idea of a separate environment is set aside. Adaptation (a one-way process) is hierarchical; co-evolution (a mutual process) is heterarchical.

Co-evolution is a process of learning for all involved. In such heterarchical situations, organizational actors have to pay close attention to others' language and behaviour and to the unfolding relationships with others. This learning might be the result of a formal negotiation or of a trust-building exercise. Or it could be the result of time spent working together. Thus heterarchical interaction encourages continuing learning about getting things done, including the learning of interactive skills like negotiation, facilitation and diplomacy. The interaction promotes adaptation and development.

Heterarchical interaction encourages continuing learning about getting things done.

38

5.5   Pluralism

It looks as if societies across the world will be increasingly pluralistic during the first part of the twenty-first century. Civil society, which is a term describing a varied set of organizations and other human associations, is taking over functions of education and culture, social integration and care, for which governments were mainly responsible in the past two centuries. The hollowing out of large organizations, achieved by out-sourcing, strategic alliances and the use of many consultants, adds to this trend towards pluralism. Single-issue pressure groups are replacing political parties as the means for mobilizing public opinion.

Big government and big corporations remain, but a smaller proportion of organizational activity is carried out within them. Immigration adds to ethnic, religious and cultural diversity. Less rigidity in gender roles and sexual orientation adds to pluralism. In a world of this kind, organizations need variety in ways of getting things done and heterarchy is a good response to this need.

5.6   Using Diverse Talents

A heterarchical organization, if it is to work properly, has to respect others' points of view, rather than trying to force everyone into a single mould. It doesn't assume that human talent comes in a single shape or size. Heterarchy is therefore a natural way for drawing on diverse talents. In the 1970s, Meredith Belbin proposed a theory of team-membership, with eight types of person having differing skills and personalities. He gave these types names like Shaper, Monitor and Finisher. Belbin's claim was that an ideal team needed all these types. A simpler proposal was made around the same time by Roberts and Fusfeld, who saw the critical work roles as Idea Generator, Champion, Project Leader, Gatekeeper and Coach.

More recently, Kate Hopkinson has described the 'Inner Skills' people deploy in organizational situations. She chooses to concentrate on skills rather than on personalities because the skills people choose vary with context. She classifies these skills into three types: *convergent* – working with what we already know and understand; *divergent* – moving away from what we currently know and understand; and *evaluative* – making decisions, choices and judgements about anything. For each of the three types there is a cool and a warm category. For example, convergence has as its cool aspects facts and figures, hard evidence and codified knowledge, while its warm aspects are communication, perception and empathy.

This gives six categories: divergent warm and cool, convergent warm and cool, evaluative warm and cool. Hopkinson's research has shown that nearly everyone has a stable ranking of his or her preferences among the six categories. For instance, an accountant might have as his first preference cool-convergent skills, with cool-evaluative skills as second preference and warm-convergent skills as the third. Someone else, say a writer of fiction, might be most confident of her warm-convergent skills, but also be happy to deploy her cool-divergent and warm-divergent skills as second preferences. A person's preferred skill sets are partly due to individual characteristics and partly to training, education and experience.

Hopkinson has found that a team functions best when the demands of the task align with the preferences of members of the team. With complex tasks, this needs variety in first preferences. But too much variety means that the team can't really work together. When the second and third preferences of some members are the same as the first preferences of their colleagues, this makes for good dialogue within the team. For example, Sue's preference for divergent skills could enable her to produce lots of new ideas. Bob likes using evaluative skills, which could help the team to see which of Sue's ideas might turn out to be practical.

But if Sue doesn't have evaluative skills as her second or third preferences, she won't be able to appreciate the value of Bob's comments, leading to fruitless conflict rather than synergy within the team.

In a strict hierarchy there are no genuine teams, so variety of this kind is impossible and a great opportunity for enhanced performance is lost. In a heterarchical organization, on the other hand, teams form naturally. Effective teamwork thus emerges easily from the heterarchical way of getting things done.

Heterarchy reduces the danger of tyranny, helps cooperation and commitment to common goals, fosters co-evolution, teamwork, learning and innovation, is pluralistic and uses diversity.

Summarizing the advantages of heterarchy, we can say that it is a bulwark against tyranny, it enables the emergence of cooperation, it generates commitment to common goals, it fosters co-evolution, learning and innovation, it is naturally pluralistic and supportive of teamwork and it makes good use of diversity.

5.7 *Advantages of Responsible Autonomy*

Several of the advantages of heterarchy also apply to autonomy. Autonomy, along with heterarchy, suits a pluralistic society and is a good way of making use of diverse talents.

A possible advantage is the avoidance of tyranny – but this is more complicated than in the case of heterarchy. If an organization is structured to give genuine autonomy to its sub-units, it will greatly reduce the danger of a tyranny imposed on these sub-units by the whole organization. But that does not necessarily prevent tyranny *within* any particular autonomous sub-unit. Domineering leaders may emerge within the sub-unit. At least we can say that if tyranny does emerge, it will be on a smaller scale than would be the case without autonomy.

There are advantages particular to autonomy. The first of these is removal of the delays and distortions that occur when a large organization tries to control everything from the centre. There are countless examples of release of energy and speeding up

41

of decisions, when central control is replaced by accountable autonomy. Invisible hands are simpler and swifter than visible ones.

The second advantage is that autonomy can be used to generate a Complex Evolutionary System. Innovation and constantly improved performance can result.

Responsible autonomy produces these advantages if the criteria are well-chosen. Too heavy a critique loses the advantage of autonomy. Too lax a critique allows self-interested actors to get away with an inaccurate picture of their performance, as happened in the case of the energy trading company Enron. Critique must avoid the dangers of Stalinism on one hand and those of Enronism on the other.

Heterarchy and responsible autonomy are two well-defined conceptual alternatives to hierarchy, and each has real advantages.

Thus, there are two well-defined conceptual alternatives to hierarchy, and each has real advantages. A deeper understanding of these triarchic alternatives may greatly improve our organizations.

6.   Cultural Theory and Triarchy Theory

6.1   Grid and Group

Twenty-five years ago, the renowned anthropologist Mary Douglas invented a typology known as Grid and Group. 'Grid' refers to an externally-imposed and formalized regulation of the actions of individuals, achieved through laws or through social discipline. 'Group' refers to membership of bounded groups, in which the behaviour of members is determined by relationships within the group.

There are four possible combinations of Grid and Group:

The four possible combinations of grid and group in society at large.

Low group combined with low grid leads to individualism, since in this situation people are not much constrained, either by rules or by relations

42

with other members of a group. The culture is one of self-sufficiency. Social interaction is through a loose network. Entrepreneurs of all kinds flourish in these conditions.

High group and high grid lead to a structured, hierarchical society. People are subject both to socially imposed roles and to control by other individuals.

High group and low grid combine to produce egalitarian social relations. Individuals exercise power only by appealing to group values and purposes. A self-sufficient Western commune is an extreme example of egalitarianism. Its cultural bias is to reject the values of the surrounding society. Members are expected to be loyal to each other.

Low group and high grid lead to a fatalistic way of life, in which people are controlled from without but themselves exercise no control over others.

Thompson, Ellis and Wildavsky developed Douglas's ideas into cultural theory. They describe individualism, hierarchy and egalitarianism as the three active ways of life. In their view, societies that fail to include any of these three active ways of life lose the wisdom associated with the excluded way. Cultural theory sees a dynamic equilibrium between the three ways, which is to the advantage of societies in which they are combined.

6.2   Parallels with Triarchy theory

Cultural theory's individualism corresponds to responsible autonomy; egalitarianism corresponds to heterarchy; both theories have hierarchy.

Triarchy theory, as expounded in this book, relates to organizations, rather than to societies, which are the arena of cultural theory. Nevertheless, there are parallels between the two theories. The three active ways of life of cultural theory correspond to the three ways of getting things done of triarchy theory. Triarchy theory postulates that there are three, and only three, ideal ways of getting things done in organizations - hierarchy, heterarchy and responsible autonomy. Cultural theory's individualism corresponds to triarchy theory's responsible autonomy, cultural theory's egalitarianism to triarchy theory's heterarchy, while both cultural and triarchy theory have hierarchy.

To recap, triarchy theory claims that, while hierarchy may have real value in organizations, a judgement about its usefulness is not possible while it has a firm grip on nearly everybody. It should first be seen as just one option. Heterarchy is described as multiple rule, rather than the single rule of hierarchy. Finally, responsible autonomy allows an individual or a group to decide what to do, but ensures accountability for the outcome of the decision. It might be called 'no rule', or rather, no external rule. The existence of accountability distinguishes responsible autonomy from anarchy.

Heterarchy and responsible autonomy are both non-hierarchical, but are distinct alternatives. Heterarchy requires strong interaction between organizational participants, in order to decide on coordinated action. The sheer density of this interpersonal communication can be time-consuming, which is a possible disadvantage for heterarchy. Responsible autonomy has less interaction and greater self-sufficiency.

Cultural theory provides a further justification for there being only three ways of getting things done and suggests a dynamic interaction between triarchy theory's three ways.

Cultural theory reinforces triarchy theory in two ways. First, it provides a further justification for there being three, and only three, ways of getting things done in organizations. The second, and more important, benefit is that cultural theory suggests a dynamic interaction between triarchy theory's three ways of getting things done. The interaction seen in society between hierarchy, individualism and egalitarianism is a possible model for what the interaction, in organizations, between hierarchy, heterarchy and responsible autonomy might be, were the hegemony of hierarchy to be removed.

Thompson, Ellis and Wildavsky suggest that people who follow a particular one of cultural theory's three active ways of life are promised particular outcomes. If, over time, these outcomes do not come about, its adherents begin to have doubts about their way of life. Eventually, they will listen to the stories told by adherents of alternative ways of life and may decide to adopt one of these. Such a switch might be manifested by supporting a different political party or reading a different newspaper.

One can see something of the sort operating in today's organizations. The frequent reorganizations that occur may not be simply whims of the hierarchy. They may be the result of dissatisfaction with the achievements of the organization and with its failure to live up to its promises. Often, today, reorganization is a shift between centralization and decentralization, or something similarly trivial, which does not seriously disturb hierarchy. But it is possible to envisage more fundamental shifts taking place when the hegemony of hierarchy is relaxed.

Thompson and his co-authors write:

The incapacities of the three active ways of life (hierarchy, egalitarianism, and individualism) prompt them to reach out for cultural allies who can compensate for their weaknesses... It is this ambivalence (being both attracted to and repelled by rival ways of life) that generates the "switching mechanisms", which continually forge, break apart and re-form alliances.

6.3   Conclusion

If the danger of hierarchical dominance were removed, one could envisage a group of people in an organization discussing how they might best cope with a new set of external uncertainties. Someone might suggest that their current practice of ample discussion of all new issues was too ponderous in this rapid-moving, new situation. If most of the uncertainties were well-understood, then quick responses would now be more important than exhaustive analysis. The group might decide to put one of their number in charge of short-term decision-making, at least for a few months. In this example, heterarchy reaches out to hierarchy as a temporary expedient in dealing with a special situation.

Although we must continue to recognize that cultural theory is primarily a theory of society, it suggests how a more dynamic triarchy theory might be developed.

7   Blending the Three Ways

7.1   Contingency Theories of Organization

The idea that the best way of getting things done will vary according to circumstances is called contingency theory.

This section is about finding the blend of the three ways of getting things done that is right for the particular situation an organization is in. It would make things easier if there were one universal way to organize. But as organizations differ so greatly in size, in their purposes and tasks, and in the technology they use, the best way to get things done is likely to vary. The idea that the best way will vary according to defined circumstances is called 'the contingency theory of organizations'. There are a variety of contingency theories. Their essence is that the effectiveness of an organization results from a good fit between its way of getting things done and the contingencies that it faces.

7.2   Donaldson's Contingency Theory

Lex Donaldson is a keen exponent of contingency theory, building on the work of earlier theorists. Over forty years ago, Burns and Stalker claimed there were two organizational styles, which they termed 'mechanistic' and 'organic'. These styles are at opposite ends of a spectrum. The mechanistic style of organization allocates people to specialized tasks and has formalized procedures and centralized decision-making. The organic style is flexible and decentralized and gives people wide responsibilities rather than specialized ones. Burns and Stalker claimed that when tasks were well defined and repetitive, the mechanistic style was best. When tasks were unclear and variable, the organic style was preferable. Their key examples were the automobile production line (mechanistic) and

46

the research laboratory (organic). Most organizations had a mixture of the two styles.

Later, Henry Mintzberg suggested an alternative spectrum, which goes from unbureaucratic to bureaucratic. The unbureaucratic style has a simple structure and centralized decision-making: people's work is non-specialized and communication is informal. The bureaucratic style is decentralized, formalized and specialized. Key examples are the owner-managed small business (unbureaucratic) and the government agency (bureaucratic).

In Mintzberg's view, bureaucracy enables decentralization. This is because it defines so carefully what everyone can and cannot do, and trains people to follow these rules. If the bureaucracy, and the systems it uses, are enabling rather than coercive then this does not have to stifle initiative. Heterarchy can be seen as extreme decentralization, and Mintzberg's argument also applies to it, since well-designed, enabling systems are of great importance for heterarchy.

After reviewing a series of academic studies carried out by himself and other researchers, Donaldson confirmed that large organizations adopt a bureaucratic style, at least for their administrative functions, while small organizations adopt Mintzberg's 'simple' style, which is more or less what experience would suggest. Similarly, he found that empirical evidence supported the idea that task uncertainty, for instance when radical innovation is the aim, requires the organic style. When there is task certainty, organizations adopt the mechanistic style.

Donaldson's model of contingency theory.

Donaldson proposed a model that combined the Burns/Stalker and Mintzberg spectra. One axis of the Donaldson model concerns decision-making: centralized to decentralized. The other axis concerns formalization: formal to informal. The result looks like this:

Bureaucratic	*Mechanistic*
Decentralized, formal	Centralized, formal
Organic	*Simple*
Decentralized, informal	Centralized, informal

We shouldn't forget that models like these deal with ideal types and can't capture the richness of actual life. Nevertheless, they are a starting point for exploring how contingencies might affect organizations' actual use of different blends of hierarchy, heterarchy and responsible autonomy.

Definition of the bureaucratic style.

The 'bureaucratic' style, typified by a government agency, will have plenty of hierarchy. Bureaucracy as defined by Weber depends on hierarchy for definition of purposes, selection of people, and resolution of disputes. Precise definition of rules, and careful training of people so they follow the rules, allows decentralization of decision-making within this style of organization. Hence, there will be a certain degree of autonomy within the bureaucratic style, and accountability will follow from its precise rules.

Strong, coercive systems, a rule-following culture and remote leadership can be expected in Donaldson's 'bureaucratic' organization, making it inflexible and uncreative. The result might be a blend something like this: hierarchy 60%, responsible autonomy 30%, heterarchy 10%. The small proportion of heterarchy arises, not by design, but from the resistance induced in people by this stifling style.

Definition of the mechanistic style.

The 'mechanistic' style of organization, typified by assembly-line production, tends to be authoritarian, so hierarchy predominates once more. People follow orders from the top, even to the extent of malicious compliance with orders they know will have a bad outcome. Leadership comes from the official hierarchy, with counter-leadership from unions or informal subversion. Power tends to be exercised overtly, justified by terms like 'the right to manage'.

The blend might be: hierarchy 75%, heterarchy (due to resistance) 25%, autonomy nil.

Definition of the simple style.

The 'simple' style, typified by a small business, might have a blend of 60% hierarchy and 40% heterarchy. The heterarchy arises when the boss isn't looking, and people get things done through informal coordination with fellow-workers.

Definition of the organic style.

The 'organic' style, typified by an industrial research and development organization, might have a blend like this: heterarchy 50%, hierarchy 30%, responsible autonomy 20%. Basic scientific research, as distinct from industrial research, would have much more autonomy in the blend.

The characteristics of Donaldson's styles can be summarized thus:

Style	Example	Hierarchy	Heterarchy	Autonomy
Bureaucratic	Government	60%	10%	30%
Mechanistic	Factory	75%	25%	nil
Organic	R & D	30%	50%	20%
Simple	Small firm	60%	40%	nil

Of course, the percentages I've suggested for these blends shouldn't be taken too seriously. They will vary from case to case, and over time, and anyway are no more than indications. Note that hierarchy makes up the biggest proportion in the blend in all but one of the four styles. This is to be expected, because the hegemony of hierarchy makes it the first choice for a way to get things done.

These four styles of organization are the basis for Donaldson's contingency theory – that is, the theory that links the effectiveness of an organization to its structure and ways of working. Although he quotes numerous empirical studies to prove his point, his studies have a rather old-fashioned air. This could be because the studies on which Burns and Stalker, Mintzberg, Donaldson and others based their theories were carried out mainly in the 1960s and 1970s. It could also be that hierarchy was so taken for granted in the organizations studied that it did not function as an independent variable. Its hegemonic grip may well have overruled the contingencies those organizations faced.

7.3   The Future of Work

Thomas Malone's book 'The Future of Work', published in 2004, aims to tell us "how the New Order of Business will shape your organization, your management style, and your life". Malone is a professor at MIT. Since the 1990s, he has carried out several large research projects with 'new economy' and traditional organizations. He identifies a three-stage trend over the last two centuries, both in society and in business. The trend is based on changes in communication technology. In Stage I, when communication depended on the horse and the sailing ship, things were generally done in small, unconnected groups. In Stage II, railways, steam ships and the telegraph allowed the rise of large groups with centralized decision-making. In Malone's Stage III, computers and the Internet are now giving us large groups with radically decentralized decision-making.

There has been a move from unconnected groups to larger groups with decentralized decision-making.

Malone suggests 'democracy' as a vital new way of getting things done in organizations. What he means by democracy is that, ultimately, decisions are made by voting. He gives the example of W L Gore and Associates, maker of Gore-Tex® waterproof fabric, which has the legal structure of a business company, but an unusual way of working.

At Gore, everyone working in the business is called an associate. Malone writes, "To become a manager, you don't get promoted, you have to go out and find other employees who will agree to work with you." He quotes an associate as saying: "A project doesn't move forward unless people buy into it. You cultivate followership by selling yourself, articulating your ideas, and developing a reputation for seeing things through." Decisions are generally made by this kind of informal consensus. Even salary decisions are made by committees, based on rankings by the person's peers.

Another example Malone gives is the well-known case of Visa International, the credit card service organization, largely created by its founder CEO, Dee Hock. Visa is a business owned by the banks it serves, and Malone calls it a 'cross-organizational democracy'. The owner-banks have voting rights proportional to the size of their credit card businesses. Simple majority votes decide many things, but certain key decisions, such as any future decision to change the name 'Visa', need as much as 80% agreement. Electronic communication makes it much easier to handle this kind of voting.

At both Gore and Visa, practices may have changed since Malone wrote about them, but the principles are still valid.

Malone also describes the process of bringing markets inside an organization. For him, the term 'internal market' means trading between organizational participants. Ultimately, decision-making is in the form of a contract, entered into through the free agreement of participants.

One example he gives is trading in CO_2 emissions between different business units within the major oil company, BP. The company has made an overall commitment to reducing these emissions. All units have to play a part in reaching the target, but some units find it easier to make reductions than others. Those that do better than average can sell their surplus to units which are struggling to reach the target. An electronic trading system allows units based anywhere in the world to trade emissions. Real money is passed from one unit to another, even though they are all within BP.

Another example comes from the electronics company Hewlett-Packard. HP has a board of senior managers that acts like a venture capital group, providing funding for projects it finds promising. Anyone in the company with a good idea can put it forward to this board. If the board says 'Yes', the champion of the idea then has to gather a project team from within HP. Unless a well-qualified team volunteers to join the project, the board withdraws funding. The willingness of people to join the project team acts as a further test of the project's viability. Therefore, as well as a market for project funding, there is a quasi-market for project team members, organized via an electronic bulletin board. (Celltech, the biotechnology company I founded in 1980, had a similar, but simpler, system.)

Malone emphasizes that these internal markets operate in much the same way as external ones. They are subject to rules, but rules determined by the company management. (External markets are ruled by law, such as the law of contract.) Internal markets are subject to regulation by an internal system, designed to prevent anti-competitive behaviour (like market manipulation), lack of transparency or failure to live up to contract obligations. Although internal rules and regulatory methods mirror external ones, they can be less elaborate, since everything happens within one company. Experience shows that honest, open and easily-understood communication is important for the operation of markets, both internal and external. It is generally easier to ensure this internally, because good communication can be supported by organizational culture and because, even in large organizations, people deal with each other more regularly than they do in external markets.

Honest, open and easily-understood communication is important for the operation of markets, both internal and external.

7.4   Malone's Contingency Theory

Malone's thesis is that low cost, easy-to-use communication, typified by the Internet, is the driving-force behind his Stage III: the wave of decentralization now happening in large organizations. This is an alternative contingency theory to Donaldson's, one in which the nature of decision-making changes with the contingency of improving communications. Although it deals only with large organizations, and is mainly concerned with the technological aspects of communication, rather than its conceptual, interpersonal or institutional aspects, Malone's thesis has the great advantage of bringing to the forefront the issue of hierarchical power. As he puts it:

When most people talk about decentralized organizations and empowerment, they mean relatively timid shifts of power within a fairly conventional, hierarchical structure.

When voting by participants is part of organizational decision-making, the grip of hierarchy is loosened, although who devises the voting system and who ensures that it is fairly used might well remain hierarchical appointments. Voting is only one of various heterarchical mechanisms – the separation of powers between different bodies and the rotation of jobs are other examples – but it is a valuable one for deciding on major matters and the *possibility* of a vote has an influence even if it never takes place. Likewise, internal markets are an important mechanism for responsible autonomy. Again, they loosen the grip of hierarchy, although it is important to consider who makes the rules for trading and who regulates the operation of markets.

Malone says that what happens in his Stage III is that organizations move from command-and-control to coordinate-and-cultivate. He stresses that coordination doesn't require control. The task of management becomes one of facilitating the organization's processes for goal-setting, standard-setting and value-articulation. **Clear purposes, high standards of performance and widespread commitment to shared values enable the organization to get things done through heterarchical interaction.** I suggest that Malone's Stage III might see organizations develop blends in which heterarchy predominates – for example, heterarchy 70%, responsible autonomy 20%, and hierarchy 10%. It would be naïve to expect that hierarchy will completely disappear.

7.5   Force-Based Organizations

Are there significant differences between organizations that depend on money and those that depend on violence?

The contingency theories of Donaldson and of Malone were developed mainly through the study of businesses, where power is particularly derived from the control of monetary resources. It is worth considering whether or not there is an important difference between organizations that depend on money and those that depend on violence, such as police forces and armies. Armies, navies and air forces, police and prison officers (also perhaps some non-state organizations like security guards) rely on the use of force. We must hope that the use of force and violence in today's societies can be rare, so force-based organizations might be regarded as exceptional, too. The force/non-force distinction might be the basis for a further contingency theory.

Force-based organizations do indeed conceive of themselves as different. Their members wear distinctive uniforms and have clear marks of hierarchy through badges of rank, gold braid, salutes and forms of address. Hierarchy is considered to be very important. A great deal of effort goes into indoctrination and training, in order to show new recruits that they belong to a special sort of organization. The work is dangerous and colleagues need to be able to rely on one another in life-threatening situations. And because their activities are dangerous to people outside these organizations, they must be particularly accountable for what they do.

The Guardian moral syndrome tells people to shun trading, to respect hierarchy and tradition, to be obedient and loyal.

Jane Jacobs, famous for her writings on cities, also has a theory about the systems of morality associated with two main groups of public occupations. In her book 'Systems of Survival', she describes these two systems as 'moral syndromes'. Within 'Guardian' occupations she groups rulership, governance, public service and force-based activities. The Guardian moral syndrome is similar to aristocratic codes of conduct. It tells people to shun trading, to respect hierarchy and tradition, to be obedient and loyal. The good soldier, whose loyalty to King and Country is paramount, is a romanticized example of the Guardian moral syndrome.

The Commercial moral syndrome tells people to shun force, to be open to innovation, to be industrious and thrifty.

The 'Commercial' moral syndrome tells people to shun force, to respect contracts, to be open to innovation, to be industrious and thrifty. The honest merchant, shrewd and inventive, who thrives through his or her wits, is a romanticized example of this syndrome. (Although Jacobs does not go into this, it seems likely that the third sector of NGOs, charities, education and so on, more or less follows the commercial style.)

Although Jacobs proposes that the Guardian syndrome applies to government in general and not only to force-based organizations, the latter provide particularly powerful examples. Jacobs' analysis supports the common-sense view that force-based organizations are different and that they are highly hierarchical.

However, this does not prove that hierarchy is good for force-based organizations, just that it is strongly entrenched in them. During World War II, the French Army and Air Force collapsed in the face of German onslaught over the six-week period starting on 10th May, 1940. Numerically – in men, tanks and artillery – the French were more or less equal to the Germans. Only in the air were the Germans superior. Almost all senior officers in the French Army were elderly and obsessed by their experiences in World War I. There was rivalry and lack of trust between the various levels of command, shown by the expectation that orders would be given in writing, even during battle. Official doctrine centred on the methodical execution of preordained plans. Very few senior officers had learned lessons from recent examples of German capabilities in Spain and Poland. If they had, they could have seen what blitzkrieg (lightning war) might be like.

When blitzkrieg struck, the French hierarchy was rigid and vulnerable to accident, such as the death of a general in a car crash or the failure of radio communication. In the French Air Force, there was continuing conflict between those officers who saw its role as supporting ground troops and those who wanted a more independent role. This confusion contributed to its early collapse. On the ground, most individual units fought bravely and sometimes were able to hold up the enemy advance, but the breakdown in command and communications, on top of training that forbade much initiative by junior officers, led to increasing paralysis. Excessive reliance on hierarchy disabled the French. Contrary to Hobbesian belief, a single powerful ruler did not automatically prevent the war of all against all. Conflict within the French Army had been hidden and under stress it emerged – with disastrous consequences.

The German Army also had a hierarchy, of course, but it was much less rigid than the French one. Williamson Murray writes about war in 1940:

*[The] Germans understood that war offered fleeting opportunities that disappeared if leaders – from general to rifleman – failed to grasp them... when necessary, artillery, infantry and other supporting branches should coordinate and act together even **without** direction from above... German commanders had to **learn** to devolve creative freedom and authority upon their juniors – an unprecedented and largely counterintuitive step. And those juniors... required relentless schooling, training and encouragement to use that freedom wisely [Original emphasis].*

A lot of responsible autonomy plus a degree of heterarchy proved superior to heavy reliance on hierarchy.

Recent military doctrine emphasizes individual initiative rather than waiting for orders from above. Perhaps in Jacobs' Guardian moral syndrome, subservience to a hierarchy should be changed to loyalty to a cause. Hierarchy might then become largely symbolic, meaning that those who are supposed to be in charge may contribute little to the organization's actual task or mission, although they might influence organizational culture. The constitutional monarch is an example. Loyalty to a flag or some other impersonal symbol might serve just as well, leading to greater responsible autonomy and less hierarchy within force-based organizations.

7.6 Size as a Contingency

Time and group size limit communication and the emergence of trust.

I will mention one further contingency: the size of the organization. In my book 'Creative Compartments', I wrote about the limit, imposed by the time needed for continuing good communication, on the number of people with whom anyone can develop a fully open and trusting relationship. This depth of trust depends on regular face-to-face contact between the members of a group. What I call a compartment is a group of people who stick together for a long time and who talk to each other a great deal. Groups of this kind can build virtuous circles in which open communication and trust reinforce each other and build to extraordinary levels.

To what size can a face-to-face group, a compartment, grow? One test is that each member of the group can recognize all the others by name. This would suggest an upper limit of a few hundred people. In his book 'Grooming, Gossip and the Evolution of Language', Robin Dunbar produced a range of biological, anthropological and historical evidence suggesting that 150 people is about the right number for a stable group. This is so whether the group is a pioneer band going out to settle a wilderness, a military unit or simply the maximum number of people with whom you can have a social relationship. Whatever the exact limit on size, it is clear that a group of this kind is qualitatively different from a larger group.

It is easier to get a robust virtuous circle going if the organization has no more than a few hundred members.

Of course, size isn't everything. It is possible to have a suspicious or strife-ridden group of a hundred people. The virtuous circles I've mentioned can be built in larger organizations. But it is easier to get the circle going, and when it is going it is more robust, if the organization has no more than a few hundred members.

7.7 Conclusion

Heterarchy may be good for Commercial organizations, while responsible autonomy may be good for Guardian organizations.

Jacobs' proposal that there are two moral syndromes – Guardian and Commercial – may point to a particularly relevant contingency. It suggests that heterarchy is well-adapted to commercially-orientated organizations, while responsible autonomy may be the better alternative to hierarchy in Guardian organizations – particularly force-based ones.

For organizations in general, size and task-certainty currently tend to determine organization style, leading to differing degrees of centralization and formality and to different blends of the triarchic ways of hierarchy, heterarchy and responsible autonomy. The communication technology available to the organization also has its effect on the blend.

8 Drivers of Change

8.1 Practical Approaches

The first edition of this book provoked considerable discussion about ways of implementing heterarchical and responsibly autonomous ways of working in practice. Perhaps the most significant of these – although also one of the most obvious – concerns how to find the impetus to achieve a shift away from hierarchy.

The question was most tellingly asked by the Managing Director of a small architecture and design practice, who had thus far run his business on hierarchical principles. His practice had been to maintain fairly close supervision of all the business's core activities as it had grown from small beginnings to employ more than a dozen professional staff. If he now chose simply to delegate his authority in different areas, how would his staff believe him? And, perhaps more importantly, how would he resist the urge to intervene if there were signs of things going wrong? If he, instead, allowed room for his staff to decide for themselves that they wanted to run the business in a more heterarchical and autonomous way, what should he do if they did not reach this conclusion themselves? Should he make it for them and enforce it? And, finally, how could he overcome the now well-established preference of his staff for him to review all key decisions, so that they would not be held solely responsible for any mistakes that were made?

There are, of course, no simple answers to these questions as they depend so much on the character and make-up of the organization and its staff. However, there are a number of practical approaches that can be taken to the subject and some of these are outlined below. Where possible, I have indicated sources of further reading, which are given in full in the bibliography.

8.2   *Ideas are Important*

I shall start by discussing the skills and institutional mechanisms that can help an organization move away from hierarchy. These skills and mechanisms are primarily needed for a move towards heterarchy, but they also support responsible autonomy, for reasons I'll discuss later.

Gustave Flaubert wrote, "I maintain that ideas are events. It is more difficult to make them interesting, I know, but if you fail the style is at fault". If in this book I have failed to persuade you of the importance of ideas like heterarchy, then it's my style that is at fault, not the ideas themselves. New ideas provide new mental models and new communication tools, which allow people to do new things. This is why ideas are so important, and why clarity and precision are necessary if novel ideas or concepts are to be effective. The ability to make ideas clear and interesting is what to Flaubert is a good style.

I shall now discuss Kenneth Cloke and Joan Goldsmith's book 'The End of Management'. I do so rather critically, because I think the authors are

Managers need to relinquish the luxury of prestige and employees need to surrender the luxury of irresponsibility.

not sufficiently clear about the concepts they use. They write of the need to transform "processes that support hierarchy into those that support heterarchy". They say that managers need to relinquish the luxury of prestige and that employees need to surrender the luxury of irresponsibility. These are aims with which I agree.

However, Cloke and Goldsmith write that every organization needs administration, coordination, facilitation and leadership. To many people these activities would be seen as 'management'. For instance, project managers usually coordinate rather than control the people involved in a project but are nonetheless called managers. So if these activities are necessary, and if they are generally thought of as management, why call the book 'The End of Management'?

The authors acknowledge that the word 'management' has various meanings. The first set of meanings is around handling things and simply coping with situations. The second set of meanings involves controlling other people, and it's the latter set they see disappearing when they talk of the end of management. I think this is unnecessarily confusing. Management in the 'handling' sense I call 'getting things done', and management in the 'controlling' sense I call 'hierarchy'. This might seem like quibbling over words. However, terminology is important, because those under the hegemony of hierarchy will use any conceptual confusion to deny the possibility of doing without it.

Cloke and Goldsmith make a distinction between organizational hierarchies and natural hierarchies. They write "...natural hierarchies are based on talent or skill, while *organizational* hierarchies are based on power and status". Again, I find this an unfortunate choice of terms. Of course, there are great variations in people's skills, but to call this a 'natural hierarchy' implies an unchanging superiority of one person over another. This is wrong because the skills needed in one situation will not be those needed in

another. I think it is be   'hierarchy' means only
'organizational hierarc

Leadership is not the same as control, power is not the same as status and management is not the same as hierarchy.

Leadership is not the s   ontrol, power is not the same as status and management is not the same as hierarchy. Conceptual confusions muddle these up and prevent us from finding better ways to get things done in organizations. I believe the confusions mostly arise from our genetic and cultural predispositions towards hierarchy, which inhibit clear thinking. When power and status are involved, concepts easily get distorted.

Although I prefer my terminology to that used by Cloke and Goldsmith, this is not my primary point. What is important is that the concepts we use are well and widely understood and are not consciously or unconsciously obfuscated for political ends.

8.3   Skills

For heterarchy, individuals need a set of skills different from those needed for hierarchy. These are interpersonal process skills, and special skills for dialogue, teamwork, mutual respect and openness.

Change in organizations requires people to acquire new skills or to develop old, latent skills. I've already mentioned one skill – clear *conceptual thinking*. This might seem to be an academic kind of thinking, but actually most people are capable of sorting out concepts when they know they are important and with the right kind of help. Look, for example, at the way people are willing to grasp the complexities of the rules of various sports. Clarity in conceptual thinking really can be acquired though training and experience.

The next set of skills is those of *interpersonal process* – listening, checking that you have been understood, negotiation, facilitation, effective participation in meetings, and so on. Probably the most advanced kind of interpersonal process is that which David Bohm calls 'dialogue'. He contrasts dialogue with debate. In debate, people present their own views and don't listen to the views of others except to score points. Dialogue, on the other hand, is a free flow of meaning between people. Bohm advocates dialogue without an agenda and without a leader, preferably in groups of twenty or more. Of course this takes time, but on fundamental issues it is time well spent.

Teamwork skills include, but go beyond, relevant interpersonal process skills. Teams are typically made up of six or seven people, but can have up to a dozen members. Teams have dynamics of their own – dynamics people can learn to understand through training and experience. Attention to both task and process is needed for effective teamwork and knowing when to shift attention from one to the other is a necessary skill. Another skill is introducing new members into a team and discovering the strengths and weaknesses of existing and new team-members. Real teams are heterarchical in their internal workings and must have a good degree of responsible autonomy in their relations with the rest of the organization – they should be given clearly defined tasks and allowed to get on with them. Skills acquired at the scale of the team can fairly easily be transferred to larger scales.

Skills for *openness* or transparency within an organization also need to be learnt, given that most people's experience is of secrecy. Internal openness often has to be combined with external secrecy – another skill.

Finally, there are the skills involved in building *mutual respect* between everyone in an organization. This may be mainly a matter of establishing a culture that puts a high value on mutual respect. But skills help here too – skills that enable people to recognize their differences from others, and to value this diversity for instrumental and humane reasons.

I would now like to discuss institutional arrangements or mechanisms that help organizations move towards heterarchy.

8.4   *Democracy*

The first of these institutional mechanisms is organizational democracy. Sometimes the term democracy is used to mean that everyone is treated with respect and that all members of an organization have a say. In this sense, democracy is similar to heterarchy.

However, it is probably more useful to define organizational democracy as voting. In this sense, democracy modifies, rather than replaces, hierarchy. In Western nations, representative democracy is the norm. A leader is elected (directly or indirectly) for a term of office of four or more years. The elected leader then governs through a hierarchy of cabinet members and civil servants. Although the consent of the governed has been given, and can be withdrawn at a future election, this is nonetheless hierarchical government.

Democracy modifies, rather than replaces, hierarchy.

With this system, many citizens see little connection between their views and the actions of the governments they elect. This contributes to poor turnout at elections and to cynicism of the kind that says: "If voting made a difference, they wouldn't let us do it". Of course, in politics, representative democracy is far better than autocracy, but it is not necessarily a good model for organizational democracy.

Direct democracy, in which voters decide on specific issues, is not widely used in politics. Referenda are rare, except in Switzerland. In the state of Oregon, in the USA, there is frequent consultation on policy. Electronic town meetings have been set up in various places. But even in these cases, hierarchical government continues.

Democracy can have an important role in making heterarchy work well in organizations.

Democracy, in the sense of voting, can have an important role in making heterarchy work well in organizations – for example, in universities and in professional service firms, like law and accounting firms. Jay Lorsch and Thomas Tierney, in their book 'Aligning the Stars', show that voting by partners in professional firms is one element in achieving effective heterarchy. Of course, in these firms, it is only one element among others, such as the development of individual talent, performance

63

reviews for everyone, task rotation, and a culture that balances individualism with collective responsibility and inspiring leadership.

What is wanted is a governance system that uses voting wisely. Lorsch and Tierney take an example from the leading New York law firm Latham and Watkins. Electing new partners to the firm is a very important matter and a great deal of effort is devoted to it. There are explicit criteria for selection, the process is driven by data not by opinion, and final decisions are made by all the firm's partners. These characteristics help to depoliticize the process. At Latham and Watkins, the partnership vote is held once a year. During the months before the vote, a consensus is built through many interviews and debates. When it comes to the actual vote, there is generally good agreement. Which is just as well, since in this firm an 85% positive vote is required to admit a partner. Without an excellent process, no new partner might ever get elected.

Carefully prepared decision-making, leading to a consensus that is eventually ratified through voting, is rather similar to the Japanese Ringi system, which I discuss in section 8.12. Processes like these ensure widespread debate and mean that everyone (at least within the senior ranks) becomes committed to whatever action is decided on. Of course, in these examples heterarchy applies only within an elite group. In the rest of these organizations, hierarchy predominates.

8.5   Separation of Powers

Political models can also be carried over into organizations, to provide a separation of powers between analogues of an executive, a legislature and a judiciary. In British universities, for example, various individuals and assemblies have powers defined by the university charter. Arrangements vary, but generally are along the following lines: the chancellor is a sort of constitutional monarch, whose official duties are mainly ceremonial, but who sometimes exercises informal influence. The vice-chancellor is the chief executive. The university council, made up of people representing local government, professional bodies, academic and administrative staff and students, has to approve key administrative appointments (for example, that of the vice-chancellor) and decisions. The chairman of council and the university treasurer, who is a member of council, have serious power. The senate, chaired by the vice-chancellor and made up of the university's academic staff, has to approve key academic appointments (for example, professors) and decisions. Finally, there is a rather remote and seldom-used body, the university court, which acts as a court of appeal on certain issues.

In practice, most things are decided by the vice-chancellor and other executives, together with the senate and the council. Committees are used to recommend decisions for ratification by the senate or council. The chair of a committee tries to make sure that its recommendations always have enough support for easy ratification. All this is complicated and often tedious, but it shows that a formal organizational heterarchy can be a long-lasting and stable arrangement.

Hierarchy-addicts dislike the importation of anything from the corrupt world of politics into the pure world of organizations.

It is hard to persuade people they can do with less hierarchy. Most people panic when they realize that the familiar way of organizing, even if it is a hated way, may disappear. Panic increases when the separation of powers is mentioned. Hierarchy-addicts particularly dislike this classic example of heterarchy, taken from the political world. They dislike the importation of anything from the corrupt world of politics into the pure world of organizations. They cite the familiar danger of gridlock. They think the separation of powers childish, nothing more than a game of rock, scissors and paper.

But most organizations already have some separation of powers. In business, the board of directors is supposed to monitor the performance and integrity of the CEO. The corporate scandals of the late 1990s have highlighted the need for this, and in the UK the currently fashionable way to make it happen is for the roles of Chairman and CEO to be separated. In not-for-profit organizations, there is often something similar, with a group of trustees or a volunteer council whose job is to ensure that the executives stick to the organization's principles and generally behave in a proper way.

In democratic countries, such as the UK, there is some separation of powers between elected (or politically appointed) ministers and career civil servants. Although the politicians have the final say, there are things that they cannot legally ask civil servants to do. As the TV series 'Yes Minister' so amusingly showed, civil servants are in fact able to use their status, knowledge and connections as a counterpoise to ministers. A further division of powers happens when an internal ombudsman is appointed.

In many organizations, there is a separation of powers between line management and staff, particularly staff responsible for matters like internal audit, safety or human resources. If a line manager overrides or obstructs such staff and something subsequently goes badly wrong, the consequences for the manager can be severe, especially when there is legal action against the organization. Likewise, if the explicit advice of recognized professionals, such as doctors or engineers, is ignored, there is a risk for the manager. A procedure for protecting whistle-blowers is a further example of separation of powers.

Some separation of powers already exists in all organizational sectors. Thus there is an existing base on which wider heterarchical moves can be built.

It is true that in all three organizational sectors – business, government and not-for-profit – measures like these may be only peripheral, leaving hierarchy as the main way of getting things done. But the examples show that at least some separation of powers already exists in all three sectors. Thus there is an existing base on which wider heterarchical moves can be built.

Here are some general suggestions about ways in which a separation of powers might be used in larger organizations.

- The first suggestion is for an expanded ombudsman function, able to investigate a wide range of possible wrongdoings – abuse of power, corruption, unfairness, discrimination, personal harassment and cover-up of mistakes. The function should have the authority and resources to respond to complaints and to initiate audits. It might be seen as an internal regulatory body. As well as having some expert staff, it should have staff posted there for a couple of years from around the organization. This would help to make the body a genuine force for good practice.

- Another possibility for the separation of powers is between setting the organization's vision, values and purpose, on one hand, and running day-to-day affairs, on the other. This would be an extension of the present separation between the duties of a board and those of the chief executive. Institutions like strategic forums could be the way to achieve this. However it is achieved, strategic work should have very clear outcomes – otherwise it is simply waffle.

- A third possibility is to separate the tasks of hiring, firing, developing, appraising and rewarding people – including many of the tasks presently done by the Human Resources function – from operations. But the staffing of the 'people group' should again include a majority of non-specialists, in this case posted in for short periods and specific exercises.

8.6   Job Rotation

There is much merit in job rotation in heterarchical organizations. It is usual in professional service firms and in universities. A professor can serve for a few years as a pro-vice-chancellor, gaining administrative and strategic experience and bringing to the post an understanding of the daily problems that the head of a department faces. Usually, this job is part-time. Similarly, within a university department, a lecturer

67

can serve for a time as sub-dean. In a law firm, the job of senior partner is often rotated, while other lawyers bring their understanding of the firm's operations to the job of chairing committees in the firm – for instance, the promotions committee.

A nice advantage of heterarchy is that the locus of effective power can so easily vary over time. Different talents can be deployed as circumstances change. For example, as a project progresses, the people who made good contributions in its early stages may not be the best suited for the later stages. In an organization with a heterarchical culture, handing around leadership will seem the natural way to do things. This is in contrast to hierarchy, which claims omnicompetence and wants the presently powerful to retain their power.

In an organization with a heterarchical culture, handing around leadership will seem the natural way to do things.

8.7   Project Leadership

Developing the theme of varying the leadership of projects over time, Nonaka and Takeuchi, in their book 'The Knowledge-Creating Company', use various sporting analogies. In a 'relay race', the baton is handed on by one individual, or team, to another as a project progresses. This method was the way product development was carried out in industry for many years. It has the big disadvantage of time delays as one team completes its task and hands over to another. Also, this sequential approach may result in no one having an overview of the whole project.

So the 'rugby' style emerged, mainly in Japanese industry, in which the ball of leadership is fluidly passed among players throughout the game. This is a self-organizing process, made possible by good training and real dedication to the overall aims of the project.

Nonaka and Takeuchi identify a third style, which they call 'American football', in which a game plan is determined for each stage. Once the game plan has been agreed, the players follow it, using rugby-style tactical cooperation within its strategic framework.

In these examples, heterarchy comes in varied blends with hierarchy or autonomy. The relay race analogy suggests mainly autonomous groups working on the separate phases of a project. When the work of one group is complete, the task is passed on to the next group. For example, in the pharmaceutical industry, a discovery group finds a promising compound, does some preliminary work on it, and passes it on to a preclinical development group. The preclinical group does more work, and then hands the baton to a clinical group for further development.

The rugby style has less autonomy and more heterarchy. Here several groups are involved on a project simultaneously, with no one group in overall control. For this to happen, everyone has to have a deep understanding of the purpose of the project.

Nonaka and Takeuchi's American football style includes an element of hierarchy, if the game plans (or strategic reviews) are controlled by coaches (or senior managers). I don't know how it is on the football field, but a hierarchy certainly isn't necessary when the American football style is followed in organizations. Strategic reviews don't need a boss. They can be done by a peer group of some kind, for instance a forum of representatives drawn from all the organization's sub-units.

8.8   Selection by Lot

In ancient Athens, selection by lot was used to choose most of the officials concerned with civilian administration. (Military leaders and officials concerned with finance were elected.) All officials were male, adult Athenian citizens. Five hundred men (chosen by lot) made up the council. A committee of five of these council members (again chosen by lot) held office for about five weeks. Every day one member of the committee was chosen to be the ruler of the state. The council as a whole kept a careful eye on the actions of the committee, and wrongful action could lead to a vote of censure, and even to banishment from Athens.

Some allocation of jobs by lot could be useful in today's organizations.

I am not advocating an Athenian style of rule for today's organizations, but some allocation of jobs by lot could be useful. For instance, consultative bodies could give guidance during the early stages of an organization's policy formulation. Their members might be chosen, by lot, from those willing to serve and willing to be trained for the work. There is an analogy here with trial jurors, who are also chosen at random, and who are supposed to bring to their task the values and experience of ordinary citizens. Just as the jury is guided on the law by the judge, guidance on technical matters could be provided to such consultative bodies by various experts.

8.9 Reward Systems

Hierarchies have systems for salaries, fringe benefits and symbolic markers of status, which are closely linked to hierarchical positions. In large organizations, a great deal of effort goes into the construction of job grades, salary scales and job evaluation. In British industry, the company car used to be a supremely important status symbol, about which vast amounts of time were spent in argument.

Heterarchical reward systems decouple reward from position in organization. They are not necessarily egalitarian – for instance, large bonuses can be paid for particular achievements – but, in a heterarchical system, decisions about the size of bonuses or other rewards have to be as objective as possible and may be made by a committee drawn from across the organization.

Decoupling reward from hierarchy avoids over-promotion to reward good service.

Decoupling reward from hierarchy avoids over-promotion to reward good service. For instance: Mary has kept the accounts accurately over many years. She enjoys doing her work and is respected for her diligence and skill. Recognizing this, she is promoted to accounts supervisor. But she has little talent for supervision and has a miserable time supervising a couple of less capable people. The end result is that three people do little more work than was previously done by one and all three are unhappy with the situation. With a non-hierarchical system, Mary could be rewarded without this unnecessary promotion.

8.10 Semco

I shall now describe an organization that has made the shift to a high proportion of heterarchy in its blend of ways for getting things done. Ricardo Semler, majority shareholder in the Brazilian company Semco, has deservedly captured the attention of the world, because of the way Semco operates and through his two lively books, 'Maverick' and 'The Seven-Day Weekend'. Semler's father handed over control of his family company to Ricardo who, at the age of 22, immediately insisted on a quasi-democratic style of management and fired those of his father's managers who didn't agree. Over the twenty years since then, Semco has been remarkably successful as a business, growing rapidly, and becoming a leader in several fields in Brazil.

There is a lot in the Semco story that I recognize from my own experience at Celltech. For example, making financial information completely open to everyone in the business and encouraging staff to analyse the monthly figures and challenge anything that isn't clear or that seems wrong. As at Celltech, such openness engenders trust in the Semco system and in Ricardo Semler as a person. Semler says trust virtually stops rumour and internal politics, which is what we found at Celltech. In both companies, people learned how to be open internally but discrete externally.

When there isn't time to consult, people at Semco act on their own initiative, reporting to their colleagues later on what they have done. Mistakes, openly admitted, are tolerated, at least if they are not repeated. This encourages learning from mistakes – what Donald Michael calls 'embracing error'. Ethical behaviour is a key part of the culture. There is also a parallel with Celltech in the size of organization. Although Semco as a whole has several thousand people, its operating units are never more than a few hundred strong.

Some things Semler writes about do not accord with my own experience. He rejects systematic ways of working, disliking procedures and planning. Of course, it is right to shun systems which don't serve the real needs of the organization and which haven't been carefully developed. But well thought-out, enabling systems are immensely valuable in providing accurate data and embedding proven practices; and people want to have them. My guess is that Semler's colleagues actually use quite a few systems of this sort, but don't make a big fuss about them, allowing him to go on believing systems aren't necessary.

Semler writes, "…I don't think we've yet managed to make democracy a reality at Semco… We make more decisions from on high than we'd like (and see them ratified at the base)…" Semler's worry might be due to unrealistic assumptions about the democratic process or a failure to distinguish between direct and representative democracy. From his descriptions, I think there is plenty of democracy at Semco, plus a wonderful acceptance of dissent and even for non-constructive dissent.

Yet Semler says he is in favour of hierarchy – although he is opposed to the things that come with it, like corner offices and reserved parking spaces – and he dislikes military organizational structures. I'm not sure how he can reconcile an apparent preference for hierarchy with his wish for more democracy. Perhaps it's connected to his continuing control of Semco through his majority shareholding. Such contradictions probably don't matter in this special case, but they would have to be resolved if Ricardo Semler wasn't such an unusual person.

Whatever the contradictions in Semler's beliefs, Semco does show that heterarchy can work extremely

well. Semler and his senior c⋯⋯ often refuse to
settle a dispute, even when as⋯⋯s to make those
involved sort it out between ⋯⋯es. Very careful
attention is paid in appointin⋯⋯ to jobs, and all
appointments need the agre⋯⋯co-workers. Job
rotation is a standard practi⋯⋯regular evaluation
of everyone's performance, conducted by peers. All of
these are great for heterarchy.

8.11 Enabling Infrastructure

Eve Mitleton-Kelly's essay, 'Ten Principles of
Complexity and Enabling Infrastructures', gives an
excellent summary of the principles of complexity
thinking and their application to organizations. She
shows how self-organization (for example, in a largely
autonomous project team) can produce novel solutions
to problems, develop new concepts and give rise to
emergent organizational forms.

One of Mitleton-Kelly's contributions to complexity
thinking is the concept of enabling infrastructure
(which can also be called enabling environment or
enabling conditions). An enabling environment has
various aspects that all support self-organization:
sociocultural, system-technical and leadership-power
aspects. An enabling infrastructure facilitates learning
and the generation and sharing of knowledge. It is
fairly similar to Malone's coordinate-and-cultivate
style of management. Mitleton-Kelly writes:

*Risk-taking is meant to help find new solutions… It is in
the nature of exploration that some solutions will work and
some will not… A good leader provides psychological space
for people to learn, but also physical space and resources
for that learning to take place.*

The skills and mechanisms I discussed above
can form part of an enabling infrastructure for
heterarchical and autonomously-responsible ways of
getting things done. A further part of the infrastructure
is a culture with an understanding of, and commitment
to, the long-term interests of the whole organization,
rather than to any sectional interests. With a culture

73

Commitment to the organization as a whole, respect, self-discipline and professional pride are all characteristics of the enabling infrastructure.

of this kind it is quite easy to avoid the self-indulgent anarchy and endless debate that hierarchy-addicts fear will be the result of any move away from their ways of getting things done. It is also quite easy to develop respect for others, self-discipline and professional pride. A widespread willingness to exercise constructive leadership can also be developed. These are aspects of an enabling infrastructure.

8.12 Participation

With heterarchy, everyone is able to get involved. This gives potential for endless talking. So how can things get done? First, it must be recognized that in a heterarchy, participation brings power but it also brings responsibility. It is no good playing at participation, expecting that eventually a hierarch will stop the game and tell people what to do. In a heterarchy, that won't happen. Secondly, decision-making must be structured, into a minimum of three phases. Phase 1 is setting the agenda – deciding which subjects should be tackled, which decisions should be made, and when. Phase 2 is setting up small groups to make detailed studies of the chosen subjects, made up either of experts, or of people representative of the organization, or of both. Phase 3 is presentation of these studies to a larger group, possibly to all members of the organization, which takes the final decision. Of course, all three phases are important – shaping the decision is as important as taking it. Lastly, there must be a reasonable degree of mutual trust between members of the organization; the way decisions are taken must always reinforce, not destroy, that trust.

The Ringi system promotes collective responsibility and gives individuals the opportunity to put forward divergent views.

An important feature of many Japanese organizations has been the Ringi system, in which key decisions must have the approval of all senior staff. This approval is given by a signature. While collecting many more signatures for a decision might seem a cumbersome process, it can, in practice, be quite straightforward once procedures are established. The organization will often be strongly hierarchical and there may be pressure from the top on those whose agreement is sought. Nevertheless, the system does promote collective responsibility and gives individuals the opportunity to put forward divergent views in a serious context.

Forums offer a similar practice to the Ringi system and can be used in conjunction with it, or independently. A forum is a regular meeting of a group of people, who can be chosen by seniority or to give a representative cross-section of the organization's staff. Up to 25 people might be involved, but around half that number will usually be more effective. The forum discusses key issues and can be used to approve key decisions. Discussion in a forum should be open, constructive and free from domination by powerful factions or interests. It can be facilitated by a member of the group or by a specialist facilitator. Careful listening is one of the norms that should become established for the working of the group.

Forums offer the opportunity to discuss key issues and can be used to approve key decisions.

Heterarchy works best when the scale is right. A mainly heterarchical organization that is doing well and growing should ask itself the question: should it split into two smaller organizations, each of which could retain its heterarchical style? The two smaller organizations would be responsibly autonomous and the relations between the two might be heterarchical. This is apparently what has happened at Semco, as it has grown. Hierarchical organizations generally don't like the idea of splitting up and use arguments about economies of scale to stop that happening. Heterarchical organizations should find it much easier to do, with a pragmatic or even experimental attitude to spinning out new, autonomous units.

8.13 Trust

Without a certain minimum of mutual trust, organizations can hardly function at all.

An organization that wants an effective heterarchy must aim for a high degree of mutual trust between its members. Indeed, without a certain minimum of mutual trust, organizations can hardly function at all, whether they are hierarchical, heterarchical or rely on responsible autonomy. Otherwise, distributed power may lead to conflict or factionalism. Mutual trust is beneficial for any organization - for a number of other reasons. First, it promotes cooperation. Secondly, it promotes innovation, because doing new things is sometimes risky and mutual trust enables people to take considered risks. Thirdly, as Bibb and Kourdi write in their book 'Trust Matters', a climate of mistrust is stressful, so mutual trust reduces stress. Finally, mutual trust promotes commitment to the overall goals of an organization. Bibb and Kourdi recommend building trust through a willingness to take personal responsibility: through admitting errors and through general consistency. Leaders with these virtues are able to create a climate of trust.

Mutual trust and complete openness on all work-related matters generate a virtuous circle.

Trust-building behaviours, like those mentioned above, are a good thing for all organizations. One particularly successful initiative is openness. In my book 'Creative Compartments', I describe how mutual trust and a practice of complete openness on all work-related matters combine to generate a virtuous circle: each reinforcing the other. Openness demonstrates to organizational participants that they are trusted to use information wisely. The lack of secrets and of hidden agendas adds to the climate of trust. Such a virtuous circle sets the scene for an effective heterarchy.

8.14 Plasticity

The Brazilian legal theorist and philosopher Roberto Unger has produced a series of works that analyse the nature of modern society and explore the possibilities for radical social change. Some of Unger's concepts may be valuable in organization studies as well as in the study of society in general.

In his book 'Plasticity into Power', Roberto Unger uses the concept of plasticity as a key way of understanding the economic and military successes of different European and Asiatic societies.

Plasticity provides the opportunity to innovate in the way production, administration or warfare is conducted.

By 'plasticity', Unger means the ease with which work relations between participants in a societal institution (including an organization of any kind) can be "constantly shifted in order to suit changing circumstances". He says that plasticity provides the opportunity to innovate in the way production, administration or warfare is conducted. Plasticity allows for variation in ways of getting things done; Unger particularly emphasizes the importance of facilitating movement away from hierarchy and of experimenting with alternative ways of getting things done. Innovations should include occasional large-scale reforms, but should also be cumulative aggregations of smaller-scale moves. Unger believes that there is no predetermined set of institutions that promote plasticity, although copying from institutions that have proved successful in different circumstances is a sensible way to proceed, if the copying is experimental and in the spirit of plasticity.

Unger finds that plasticity has increased with two factors: the first of these is a reduction in the distinction between the roles of task-definition and task-execution, which is, roughly speaking, the distinction between those who manage and those who do the work. Allied to this is a reduction in the distinctions between different work-roles: between those of the specialist and the generalist; between those of the expert and the enthusiast; between staff and line.

The second factor is not part of the immediate organizational setting (whether of production, administration or warfare) but concerns the larger framework of institutions (public and private) within which work organizations have to function. According to Unger, the softening of established social roles and of hierarchies in the wider society promotes plasticity within that society's organizations.

Unger's arguments for plasticity as the basis for societal success are based on numerous historical examples. These appear mainly in the volume entitled 'Plasticity into Power', which is part of the three-volume work 'Politics'. The breadth of Unger's examples and the clarity of his analysis are compelling.

8.15 Things that Help Heterarchy

This is a summary of the things that help heterarchy in organizations:

- We think we understand hierarchy, although its hegemony is seldom recognized. But the idea of heterarchy is a mystery to most people, including its relationship to concepts like leadership, control, power and status. A much better understanding of the idea is vital.

- Individual skill sets must be developed that are different from those needed for hierarchy. Heterarchy needs general skills for interpersonal process, and special skills for dialogue, teamwork, mutual respect and openness.

Institutional mechanisms useful for heterarchy are: democracy through voting, separation of powers, job rotation, selection by lot, non-hierarchical reward systems and proper structuring of decision-making.

- Institutional mechanisms that can be valuable include: democracy through voting, separation of powers, job rotation, selection by lot, non-hierarchical reward systems and proper structuring of decision-making.

- Heterarchy works best when the size of the organization is small enough to permit skill in interpersonal process.

- A dedication to increasing plasticity in organizational arrangements.

8.16 Things that Help Responsible Autonomy

Mitleton-Kelly remarks that connectivity (meaning interaction between organizational participants) cannot be increased indefinitely without breakdown. Heterarchy must stop somewhere. The boundary of the organization is one obvious limit. But in large organizations there will have to be other boundaries. This is where responsible autonomy comes in – ways have to be found to divide up the organization into chunks, which have as much natural autonomy as possible.

Decisions about the boundaries of autonomous sub-units, and about the encapsulation of the sub-units, can be hierarchical or heterarchical. But once autonomous units have been established, and their responsibilities agreed, they have to operate under the encapsulating rules.

Moving towards greater autonomy is in most ways simpler than moving towards greater heterarchy. Here are some guidelines for moves to responsible autonomy:

- First, ask the question: is autonomy the right way to go, rather than seeking better heterarchy? Autonomy may be simpler, but will it get things done in the way the organization needs?

- If responsible autonomy indeed seems the way to go, then look at scale. Is it right to give autonomy to a small, self-organizing team? Or would a compartment with up to a few hundred people be the right size? Or is a still larger sub-unit a better size for the tasks involved, in spite of the dangers of too much interaction? Are there limits to growth for the autonomous unit, or could small turn into large without causing problems?

- Whatever the scale, the next thing to work out is the mode of encapsulation. The boundaries of the autonomous unit's field of action and responsibilities need to be carefully defined before it sets off on its self-organizing path. Of course, as time goes by, these boundaries can be renegotiated but the clearer the boundaries are, the easier any renegotiation will be. For autonomy to be genuine, renegotiation must be a heterarchical process.

- Critique must be put in place from the start. The autonomous unit has to know how it will be

79

held to account. What information will it have to provide regularly to the wider world? What are the criteria for success and failure? When will audits or reviews be held, how will these be organized and who will be involved? It's careful thought at the beginning that makes autonomy succeed.

- A key skill for any organization that is serious about responsible autonomy is in drawing up contracts for autonomous units, in such a way that the contract can be easily and fairly monitored. An organization can develop this skill through a policy of explicit contracting, even in small matters and even if the practice is a small-scale one. Performance criteria have to be mutually agreed and a good habit is to define criteria for success whenever a decision is made or a policy established. Furthermore, contracts and conventions are also important as these often act as constraints that limit social dynamics in complex situations (see below).

- As discussed above, the actions of organization members are shaped to a high degree by the existence of specific, enabling organizational structures and infrastructures. Moving away from hierarchy does not mean abandoning structures. Indeed, in many ways, clear and effective structures are more important than ever during the transition, just as they might be for an individual seeking to move away from a dependency on addictive behaviours or substances. Of course, as part of the move away from hierarchy, it is important that the structures be mutually agreed rather than imposed by the outgoing hierarchy.

- The provision of psychological space and freedom, together with physical space and resources, is necessary for learning and emergence to occur in any organization. This is nowhere more important than in the move towards responsible autonomy. Physical changes are often required to mirror and demonstrate the conceptual change in organization structure and to permit the emergence of new thinking and new behaviours.

- The eighth of 14 points proposed by W. Edwards Deming, the father of Total Quality Management, was the need to 'drive out fear'. Deming saw management by fear as counter-productive in the long term, because it prevents workers from acting in the organization's best interests, and we have already established that fear is one of the unspoken tools of hierarchy. Emancipation from domination and human freedom are important in overcoming the deadening grip of hierarchy and particular care needs to be paid to creating systems and structures that are more powerful and resilient than the ingrained habits of coercion and bullying that can underpin hierarchical management. The same is true of the need to endorse systematically individual rights in the face of powerful group interests.

- Lastly, a procedure for the resolution of disputes should be set up. This does not have to be anything complicated – it might be agreed that a single trusted individual should adjudicate.

Enabling infrastructure, encapsulation and critique are the key concepts for responsible autonomy. Skills for individuals include team-working, openness and boundary-spanning. Mechanisms include capsule-building, establishment of critique and dispute-resolution.

To summarize the things that form part of an enabling infrastructure for responsible autonomy:

- Clarity of concepts is vital for successful responsible autonomy (and for heterarchy, too). Enabling infrastructure, encapsulation and critique are the key concepts.

- Individual skill sets include some of those also needed for heterarchy, such as team-working and openness. Skill in boundary-spanning is particularly important.

- Mechanisms include capsule-building and establishment of critique and of dispute-resolution.

9   What is to be Done?

9.1   The Time is Ripe

There is a mass of evidence to suggest that, in the twenty-first century, the time is ripe for sustainable change in the methods organizations use to get things done. This will probably result in continuing moves away from hierarchy in organizations.

The knowledge economy, improved communications, external critique and the entry of more women into hierarchies all make the move away from hierarchy easier.

First, the much-heralded knowledge economy depends totally on knowledgeable people, who will not easily submit to the old hierarchical ways. The greater numbers of well-educated people, certainly in the developed world and increasingly in the developing world, mean that knowledgeable people and knowledge-intensive organizations will become the majority. Manuel Castells writes that an emerging Network Society is displacing hierarchy. Philip Bobbitt proposes that the nation-state is giving way to what he calls the market-state, in which numerous and diverse organizations reduce the role of hierarchical government.

Secondly, increasing computer power and cheaper communications mean that organizations have much more dense interconnections than before. These are both internal connections and external ones. (This is the point made by Tom Malone and discussed in Sections 7.3 and 7.4.) Good communications can replace much of the coordinating role previously claimed for hierarchy.

Thirdly, the increase in external critique, both from sensation seeking media and from better considered analytical and certificatory sources, means that bad practices and their outcomes cannot be hidden as they used to be. The poor performance of many hierarchies will be exposed.

Fourthly, the entry of women in good numbers into most organizational hierarchies might make it slightly easier to reduce hierarchy for its own sake. I say *slightly* easier, because, in many ways   may be just as addicted to hierarchy as men.

9.2   How to Change

Hierarchy is chosen irrationally.

In this book, I hope I have made the   we humans have an addiction to hierarchy, based in our genes and reinforced by a long cultural tradition. This way of getting things done is an irrational choice – whether or not hierarchy is efficient, we choose it anyway. I hope I have also made the case that heterarchy and responsible autonomy are good alternatives to hierarchy, and that they are already in widespread use in organizations. Organizations use blends of the three ways of getting things done, and these blends differ with circumstances. Finally, I hope I have convinced readers that an awareness of hierarchy's present hegemony would allow its usefulness to be judged objectively. I believe that moving away from hierarchy would improve the effectiveness of most organizations.

Sustainable organizational change must be non-hierarchical.

Sustainable organizational change can only take place in a non-hierarchical manner. Imposed change, which ignores the need for learning and overrides personal values, cannot work for long. Worthwhile change only emerges from reflective practice and has to be fully embraced by all concerned. The load of ill-considered changes, which hierarchical organizations must presently endure, can be avoided by a heterarchical approach.

Readers who have got this far in the book may feel like asking a number of questions. For instance: how do hierarchy, heterarchy and responsible autonomy interact within an organization? In other words, what are the mechanics of triarchy? How and why do blends of the three ways of getting things done change over time, in response to circumstances and contingencies? Can the interaction of the three ways somehow be modelled? These are excellent questions, but I don't feel able to answer them. The reason for this is the hegemony of hierarchy.

Because hierarchy's hegemony is presently all-pervasive in organizations, and because the use of its two alternatives is undeveloped, our experience of the interaction between them and hierarchy is quite limited. Therefore, at this stage, it would be too speculative to construct a model of their interaction – although in years to come, I hope a model of this kind will become possible and useful. What we need now is to take the alternatives seriously and to use them in practice.

Because durable change cannot be imposed, and only emerges from successful practice, it does not make sense to look for a cast-iron prescription for change towards heterarchy and autonomy. So the only agenda for change I can offer is taken from two potential role models (described in Section 9.3) and four stories (Sections 9.4-9.7). I hope that the examples that now follow will help and encourage readers to think of changes that might work well in their own organizations. The ideas explored here are summarized in a list in Section 9.8.

9.3   Role Models

In section 8.4, I discussed organizational democracy as a mechanism that helps moves towards heterarchy. I mentioned democratic practices in professional partnerships, such as legal and accounting firms, in order to demonstrate that these practices are fully compatible with business success, on a small or a large scale. This sometimes leads to the valid objection that many such partnerships are highly hierarchical and that employees in them often find them far from democratic. But I am not suggesting that these firms are in general ideal role models for heterarchy, even though some of the practices in particular firms may be worth copying.

So, where should we look for role models? Role models are of limited use, since each organizational situation has its own demands and copying what has worked somewhere else will not necessarily be useful.

But we probably want them as guides and I will present two rather different organizations with this aim in view.

A case study showing the progression from hierarchy to responsible autonomy and then to a combination of heterarchy and responsible autonomy at BP.

The first is the major oil company BP, one of the largest organizations in the world, at least in financial terms. In writing about BP, I draw on John Roberts' excellent book 'The Modern Firm' as well as on my own knowledge of the company, gained from informal contact with its staff and with other people in the oil and chemical industries.

Roberts agrees with other observers in giving much of the credit for a successful organizational form to John Browne, who became CEO of BP in 1995. However, Roberts recognizes the contributions of other BP executives, so his is not simply a 'great man' story. This is just as well, because such stories have a habit of proving premature in the light of subsequent deterioration. In the case of BP, the more recent series of safety and environmental disasters, mainly in its US operations, have blackened the company's reputation and that of John Browne. Maybe the downside of responsible autonomy is that some managers don't accept responsibility in the round, but only for those things that they think are being scrutinized. An alternative explanation is that safety performance did not figure explicitly in the remits of business area managers.

At the end of the 1990s, Browne was responsible for the exploration and production activities (E&P) of BP. He and others had seen that smaller, entrepreneurial firms were better at finding new sources of oil and getting them into production than were the major companies. The majors had superior financial and technical resources, but were not able to deploy them as effectively as their entrepreneurial competitors.

Browne looked for a way of organizing a large company that could capture some of this entrepreneurial spirit. The old BP E&P organization had numerous committees and complex systems for approval of expenditure and of other decisions. The new organization had a small executive committee (Browne and two others), to which reported twenty or so 'asset managers'. 'Asset' was a term with a less bureaucratic feel than the more conventional 'business unit'. An asset might be a single oil field. Between the Executive Committee and each asset manager was an explicit contract, under which the manager undertook to deliver a well-defined performance. Providing the contract was fulfilled, the asset manager had great freedom to operate without interference from central staff. Managers could hire and fire their own staff and use external resources rather than BP departments, if they wished. The former central staff was reduced nearly to nil, partly by redeployment into the assets.

The new organization started to deliver good results within a few years. However, it was clear that improvements could be made. The slimming down of central staffs meant that asset managers could not easily get help when faced with business or technical problems. To fill this gap, 'peer groups' of asset managers were created. Four or five managers formed a group, the members of which gave each other help when asked. The groups were formed with members who faced similar tasks, for example, there was a group of assets where the main task was to find new oil. Peer groups shared examples of good practice and, later on, 'peer challenge' was introduced, in which peers scrutinized the contracts between managers and the executive committee. Peers were able to point out areas in which more demanding targets might be possible. This 'raised the game' of the whole peer group. Later still, peer groups took on responsibility for allocating capital spending within the group. This structure affected the whole organizational culture in E&P. There was great emphasis on performance, on mutual trust and mutual help, and on admitting to mistakes and difficulties at an early stage.

John Browne is a forceful personality. This, together with his hierarchical position, enabled him to introduce a novel, and possibly risky, organizational structure quite rapidly. Browne was the boss and his ideas were followed. He was probably helped by the professionalism of BP's E&P staff, who may have recognized that his ideas were sound. Having successfully climbed the corporate ladder, Browne may have believed that hierarchy was the way to get things done. But the performance of BP's smaller competitors had to be explained and their reliance on responsible autonomy, rather than hierarchy, was one explanation. So Browne decided to hand over much of his power to the asset managers. They would be held accountable for performance, but they had freedom to decide how they would perform. So hierarchy gave way to responsible autonomy as the most important organizing principle in BP's E&P arm.

Hierarchy may have helped at the start, but, once responsible autonomy took over as the guiding principle, the 'assets' were given operating freedom and explicit contracts. A few years later, the emphasis shifted to heterarchy, as the peer groups were formed. A good deal of power and responsibility was devolved to these groups, and their mutual trust was a key feature of their successful heterarchical interaction. Asset managers were members of peer groups. They were in many ways responsible to the peer group of which they were a member.

When Browne became CEO of BP as a whole, he introduced the structure that had worked so well in E&P across the company. BP had previously been a cumbersome bureaucracy, with a complex matrix structure. This had been simplified under successive CEOs, but giving radical autonomy to the assets (now called 'business units') was a big change. In his book, Roberts uses the term 'disaggregation' to describe the process of "creating relatively small sub units within the organization in which significant decision rights are lodged". Routines and processes are such as to hold the sub-units responsible for delivering performance. Financial reporting was switched to make the assets rather like independent companies. Other management information was disaggregated so that asset performance was highlighted.

In the late 1990s, BP made several large acquisitions, most notably the US oil companies Amoco and Arco. Large mergers often fail to meet the objectives set when the deal is done. But BP's deals have all worked well. Roberts writes:

It is arguable that the value created in BP's acquisitions of Amoco and Arco came from applying BP's superior management systems to the physical and human resources of the acquired firms.

Separating leadership from hierarchy at W L Gore.

Another role model is the company discussed in Section 7.3 of this book: W L Gore, makers of Gore-Tex® waterproof fabric products. In the BP example, the most interesting feature is the progress from hierarchy to responsible autonomy and then to a synergistic combination of responsible autonomy and heterarchy. In the Gore example, the key feature is the beneficial separation of leadership from hierarchy. The company's success depends on distributed leadership and the culture of the company is such that this leadership is respected and followed. It is not necessary to have job titles and organization charts for leadership to be effective. At Gore, leadership is thoroughly professional. Projects are well thought out and well presented. Project champions are not able to gather support from co-workers unless this is so. As support accumulates for a project, it becomes better and better defined: for instance, as people skilled in project accounting join the team, as well as those with relevant marketing or technical experience. Projects inevitably compete for key people and other resources, and there is rivalry between them. However, priority choices are made heterarchically. Again, the long-established culture of the company helps this work. People are reasonable when pushing their own projects since they hope others will be reasonable in future. Also, heterarchical negotiation over resources is a skill that has developed over the years.

As effective heterarchies partly depend on a supporting culture in the organization, it takes some time to get them established. This is why a strong and determined leader like John Browne at BP can be important in moving to heterarchy. Alternatively, a small, well-motivated executive group could play this role. Either way, there is something of a paradox. The use of hierarchical power can, at first, impose the dispersed power of heterarchy.

9.4   The Centre for Computational Biology

A new organization might be a good place for a different blend of the three ways of getting things done. Whoever founds a new organization, there will be other stakeholders – funders, people who will work in the organization, potential customers or suppliers, possibly regulators – who will be interested in its effectiveness. If stakeholders are involved in its design, an unconventional organizational design won't later on come as a surprise. This theme is explored here, in the first of my four stories about organizational change.

A heterarchical approach to the establishment of a new research centre.

In the 1980s, the University of Barchester was approached by a wealthy medical research foundation, which wanted to fund research that combined molecular biology with information technology. After a series of meetings, the university agreed to found a Centre for Computational Biology. Substantial funding was guaranteed by the foundation for five years, with a promise that this would continue in later years if the Centre were successful. It was agreed that its Governing Council would include members from the university and the foundation, as well as independent scientists in the fields of biology and computing.

An early task for the Council was to attract promising scientists to the Centre. The traditional way would have been to choose someone with an established reputation as the Centre's director and let him or her recruit the rest of the staff. But the Council decided on a heterarchical approach. There were to be three senior scientists in the Centre, who would all join the Council. The three would all be paid the same and would have research groups of around ten people

89

each. To handle administration and to represent the Centre within the university and externally, one of the senior scientists would be appointed as Head of Centre. This post would be held for two years in rotation. There would also be an administrator for the Centre who would report to whomever was Head of Centre.

Although having a Head of Centre sounds hierarchical, the holder of the post consulted the other two senior scientists on any important administrative matter. The three operated as a heterarchy. For their own research they had autonomy to choose their programmes and to select their staff. They were accountable to the Council for doing good research, but how they did it was up to them. Whichever of the three was Head of Centre was accountable for proper administration to the Council, to the university and to the foundation.

There was some hierarchy – the senior scientists were bosses of their own groups, although their personal scientific skills were the real source of their authority, not their formal positions. The administrator reported to the Head of Centre, but in practice had a lot of autonomy, as the Head wanted to spend as much time as possible on his or her own research, and as little as possible on administration. After a couple of years, a further bit of heterarchy was introduced when the Council decided to add to its membership one of the post-doctoral scientists working in the Centre, recognizing that staff were a stakeholder group which should be represented on the Council.

The Centre proved to be very successful. All three senior scientists achieved international recognition within the first five years of the Centre's existence. The foundation extended its funding for a further seven years and the Centre continued to operate with the minimum of organizational fuss and the maximum of high-quality science. The Council felt that their early decision to go for lots of heterarchy and autonomy had played a big part in the Centre's success.

9.5   TS plc

The shift towards heterarchy can be triggered by an external event and enabled by a culture of trust.

In 1998, Technology Solutions plc (TS) was spun out of a financial institution. This institution, which managed one of the largest private equity funds in the City of London, had during the previous five years acquired control of many medium-sized precision engineering companies. Mostly, these were pretty sound businesses that had been bought out from conglomerate groups. The original idea was to sell these on or to float them as independent businesses but, in the dot-com frenzy of the time, investors were desperate to shift into e-business, and precision engineering was scorned as 'old economy'.

Rather than trying to sell 14 separate businesses, Alistair Scott, a senior executive in the financial institution, persuaded his colleagues that the businesses could be packaged together and floated as a single company. It would still be classed as an 'old economy' company, but it would be large enough to get the attention of the City. The flotation turned out to be reasonably successful, and TS became a separate business, with Scott as chairman.

Because they had been intended to be sold one-by-one, the businesses within TS had been kept as largely autonomous units. Scott thought about how to make the whole of TS into more than the sum of its parts. Good accounting systems were already in place, and TS had recruited a Chief Financial Officer (CFO) who was well liked in the City. Beyond this, the common factor between TS's businesses was that they provided innovative technological solutions for particular problems encountered by makers of quality equipment of many kinds. The keys to success were technical knowledge of a high order and speedy execution.

As knowledge was a key factor, Scott recruited a Chief Knowledge Officer (CKO) for TS, to join the CFO and himself as the three senior people at the centre. The newcomer realized that the knowledge TS needed mostly couldn't be codified, as it was tacit knowledge in the heads of the engineers in its companies. So managing knowledge had to be about putting people with problems in touch with people who might have solutions. Also, it had to be about developing trust between people, so they were willing to share their knowledge. The CKO set up a system that enabled TS people to make contact with colleagues who might have relevant knowledge. After two years, TS saw an unexpected bonus – posting people between its companies started to happen in a self-organized way, as new projects started and old ones finished. This was because the practice of knowledge exchange had built up mutual trust and accurate understanding of individuals' capabilities.

When the dot-com bubble burst, less glamorous businesses like TS came back into fashion. In 2001, a large American conglomerate made an offer for three of TS's companies. In financial terms, the offer was too good to refuse. But it caused a crisis within the group. What was the point of building up trust, effective communication, and mutual reliance across the group if these could be casually sacrificed for short-term financial gain? Alistair Scott reacted by calling an all-day meeting of the CEOs of TS's 14 companies, also attended by the group CFO and CKO.

Scott had encouraged openness and, at the meeting, opposing points of view were openly and vigorously expressed. The financially-oriented view was that shareholder value must prevail. If it did not, the City would lose confidence, TS's share price would fall and the group would be ripe for takeover. The opposing view was that the only way to build long-term shareholder value was through superior technology, and that needed the kind of knowledge exchange that TS had begun to develop so well. Surely it was possible to convince the City that this made sense.

After much discussion, one CEO spoke up. She was the head of one of the companies the US group wanted to buy. "I'd much rather stay in TS," she said. "But, the price we're being offered is already good, and if we negotiate hard could probably be improved. The cash you'd get would strengthen TS and allow it

92

to flourish. I'd go for the deal." This met with general approval. Alistair Scott thanked everyone for their plain speaking. He promised that the kind of dialogue they'd seen today would continue.

The deal was done at a good price. Part of the money received was returned to shareholders, part invested in the remaining businesses. The City was delighted. Scott consulted his board of directors, who agreed that the meeting of group CEOs should become a regular forum for group strategy. The board agreed it would usually support any decision the forum reached, provided it was done through careful dialogue. Scott continued as board chairman, but on a non-executive basis. His other main tasks were to chair the forum and to convince investors that this heterarchical mode of governance was genuinely in their interests. The CFO and CKO remained very influential, but their voices did not dominate.

TS's companies retained their autonomy, although if any company's performance fell short it received serious critique from the forum. This could result in swift action, initiated by a special committee appointed by the forum, and sometimes led to the management of the defaulting company getting fired. Heterarchical rule was not a soft option. Autonomy for the companies meant that each decided how it would get things done, within the group's overall policies for financial control and knowledge exchange. After a few years the group's pattern for heterarchical rule was adopted within most of the TS companies, who set up mini-forums of their own.

The TS story suggests that change towards reduced hierarchy can be triggered by an external event. However, such changes may not be effective without a compatible cultural background. In the case of TS, the shift to a more heterarchical rule was enabled by the culture of trust and mutual support that had developed through practice in knowledge exchange, helped by Alistair Scott's leadership.

9.6 Save the Planet

Selection by lot and an autonomous approach to decision-making may also require a system of relatively tight checks and balances.

Save the Planet UK, a campaigning organization dedicated to environmental sustainability, has a membership of more than 30,000. Eighty percent of its income comes from members' subscriptions and donations. Members volunteer for office help, are active in fund-raising, and turn out for demonstrations. A couple of years ago, Barbara Sim, director of Save the Planet, realized that there was a curious lack of involvement of the membership with most of what the organization did. The board of trustees were members, of course, but there were only a few of them and they were mainly elderly and distinguished. Much the same applied to the advisory panels on topics like global warming or farming practices. Research and campaign planning was done by the staff in the London office, with little input from the members around the country.

Barbara wanted to change this. She wanted to attract 'the average member' to a newly formed council of some kind. Other membership organizations try to do this by well-publicized elections of council members, but the election process seems to put off lots of people. Barbara thought a lottery might work better. Anyone who had been a member for a qualifying period of three years could say they were willing to serve. A random choice would then be made from among all those who had put themselves forward. All those chosen would have to go on a three-day training course. They would serve on the Save the Planet Council for around three years. Periods of service would initially be staggered, so that one third of the members would retire each year.

Barbara discussed these ideas with the Trustees. She suggested that the Trustees should remain responsible for financial prudence and probity at Save the Planet. The new Council would approve policies proposed by herself and her staff. The Trustees and the Council would be jointly responsible for staff matters, particularly the appointment of the director. The Trustees generally agreed and the idea was floated in Save the Planet's Newsletter. Eventually it was approved at the annual conference of members.

Over a hundred names were put forward, from which twelve were chosen at random. This novel way of selecting a governing body attracted a lot of media publicity, some of which was favourable, some not. The publicity certainly made members feel involved and recruitment of new members jumped. The Council decided it would have sub-committees to concentrate on particular issues. For the first eighteen months everything was fine.

Then came the fuel protests. A combination of tax increases and a general rise in the cost of crude oil caused diesel fuel prices to increase by about 25%, leading to direct action by road hauliers, who blocked the transport of fuel from refineries. The resulting fuel shortages were very unpopular and the government, backing away from its previous green rhetoric, made concessions to the hauliers. Some of the members of the Save the Planet Council were furious. If polluters could get their way by illegal action, shouldn't the good guys do the same?

The Council sub-committee on recycling was already impatient with the lack of progress in educating the general public to stop chucking their paper, glass, tins and other rubbish into one big bin, and to be willing to pay the cost of effective recycling. Staff members pointed out that numerous surveys showed that public opinion was steadily shifting in the right direction and that politicians were reacting to this shift. Progress seemed slow at the moment, but it was reasonable to expect big changes in a few years time.

That wasn't good enough for the Council sub-committee. They got together with a local supporters group in South London and arranged a series of blockades of the entrance of a large, newly constructed and unpopular incinerator. Their aim was to dramatize the case that incineration was an inferior substitute for proper recycling. The blockades were well planned and pretty effective. With nowhere for it to go, rubbish piled up in local neighbourhoods. This turned popular feeling against Save the Planet, spurred by faltering appearances on TV by some sub-committee members.

Barbara Sim was abroad, at a world conference on sustainable development. When she realized what was going on, she flew home, and on arrival saw a two-page article in a usually supportive Sunday broadsheet – headlined 'Can Save the Planet Save Itself?' – which blamed this 'disaster' on the 'crazy' way the organization chose its Council members. Over the next few days, she gave several press and radio interviews in which she apologized for what had happened, said that direct action had now stopped, explained that it was an isolated initiative that had, unusually, not been properly thought through, and that incineration was nonetheless a bad way of dealing with waste. The media moved on to other targets and the crisis was over. After a couple of months, popular support for Save the Planet seemed as high as ever.

All the same, Barbara realized that she had initiated something that lacked checks and balances. Following discussions with the Trustees, the Council and staff, Save the Planet adopted something like the Japanese 'Ringi' system. Before implementation, policy initiatives needing significant time and money, or with serious media implications, had to be signed off by a group of 'elders' – fifteen or so people chosen from experienced staff and savvy Council members. The elders were nominated by Barbara and her choices approved by both the Trustees and the Council.

Barbara also proposed that the Council should have a small support staff of its own, to help it work up its initiatives in some detail before presenting them to the rest of the organization. This ran the risk of generating conflict between the Council and its own little staff on one hand and the bulk of Save the Planet's staff on the other. She asked the Trustees whether they would take on a mediating role if any of these conflicts got serious. These ideas were implemented. Save the Planet thus got a simple version of the separation

of powers of political theory. The staff made up
the executive, the Council was a kind of legislature
and the Trustees were a judiciary ready to step in to
resolve disputes.

9.7   The London Classical Orchestra

**The introduction of a
heterarchical approach
may lead to some delays
and bottlenecks, but is
ultimately beneficial.**

Throughout the world, most major cities have a
single prestige orchestra, with a famous conductor
worshipped by a circle of wealthy donors. London
is unusual in that it has four symphony orchestras
battling for local audiences, for recording contracts
and for appearances in other parts of the UK and
abroad. The London orchestras survive through their
adaptability and musical entrepreneurship, not by
having superstar conductors.

The London Classical Orchestra (LCO) has had much
the same structure for the past fifty years. It is self-
governing, with the ultimate decisions being made
by the players themselves – about eighty of them.
The players elect an Executive Committee of eight
members, drawn from all sections of the orchestra,
and the Committee itself elects its Chairperson.
The Committee appoints a Managing Director, who
recruits staff to look after matters like concert and
recording production, marketing and PR, the logistics
of moving the orchestra to distant venues and the
personnel function. The last is important, particularly
because freelance players have constantly to be
brought in for specific works, or to cover sickness and
other absences.

The Managing Director and other administrative
people have a certain authority over members of the
orchestra. Producing a concert is quite a complex
job. Systems are needed to ensure that it happens and
people have to follow them. Above all, players must
turn up, without fail, for every rehearsal, concert
or recording session, or else they must organize a
reliable, fully-qualified substitute.

The orchestra also has to attract the best conductors it can. It usually appoints a Principal Conductor, and up to four more with titles like Conductor Emeritus or Principal Guest Conductor. These are people who are willing to have their names linked semi-permanently with the LCO and who agree to conduct between two and fifteen of its concerts each year. These conductors may be attracted to the LCO as their 'tame band' for recording contracts, or because they want a secure base in London from which to develop an international career. Some conductors play a role in developing the orchestra's general musical capability. Others simply agree to conduct a particular concert programme, training the orchestra for that programme only.

In musical interpretation, the conductor of course takes the lead, although members of the orchestra are not afraid to make suggestions. This could be seen as a hierarchical relationship, but since the orchestra appoints the conductor, it is only temporarily hierarchical. The principals of the various sections of the orchestra have a big say in what happens in their sections, and the orchestra's leader has an overall role in recruitment and development of its musicians. But again this semi-hierarchical role is tempered by the fact that ultimate decisions are made by the whole orchestra. What counts the most is that the performance of everyone – conductor, leader, principals, and players – is plain for all to hear and see. Failure by someone newly recruited cannot be hidden, even if he is the nephew of a famous singer or she has a pretty face.

Recently, London orchestras have found things even more competitive. They have had to look for more out-of-town work, making logistics and personal travel more complicated. To cope with this, the LCO's members decided to set up a computerized system they could access via the Internet. This would give them up-to-date information about future concerts, the venues and who was playing in them.

A group of twelve people agreed to work with the designers of the system in a pilot exercise. They sorted out various problems and brought back key decisions for the whole orchestra to decide. For instance, should the system include provisional bookings or only confirmed ones? Eventually this group was satisfied that the system was sufficiently user-friendly, and it was introduced after further consultation with the orchestra. This was a time-consuming way of doing things, which limited the number of new systems that could be considered, but members felt they were in control: it wasn't possible to grumble about what 'they' were doing. In the LCO, 'they' were 'us'.

9.8 Heterarchical Practices Illustrated by These Stories

- Rotating the position of director every few years, within a small group of senior people.

- In a smaller organization, making final decisions on key matters in meetings of all members.

- In a larger organization, sharing knowledge through a system for the identification of knowledgeable individuals and by building a climate of trust.

- In a larger organization, having a forum for strategy made up of representatives from sub-units.

- In a larger organization, having a 'Ringi' system for authorization of new initiatives.

- Trying out new systems within a panel of user representatives.

- Having representatives of all stakeholders on a governing council.

- In a membership organization, selecting members of a governing council through a lottery.

- Using a separation of powers.

9.9   Conclusion

Hierarchy is so entrenched that a complete replacement, if it does prove desirable, will take centuries. Long-term change has to be achieved through lots of smaller, shorter-term changes. And these smaller changes should emerge from local learning, rather than being laid down in external blueprints. Nevertheless, in conclusion I can suggest four guiding principles:

- **Understanding**
  If we really understand the grip hierarchy has on human beings, and know what the alternatives are, then we will be far more likely to move confidently away from hierarchy towards combinations of heterarchy and autonomy. We also need to understand that the world is complex – simplicity is appealing, but it can be misleading and sometimes dangerous.

- **Innovation**
  Imagination, experimentation and persistence will enable us to discover all kinds of novel institutions and new practices for getting things done. The hope that hierarchy (in the form of a Great Man, Great Woman or whatever) will solve our problems has often hidden the need for organizational innovation.

- **Balance**
  Heterarchy is balance, and moves towards it should be balanced, too. Innovation should be tempered with stability. What is best in the long run should be balanced against what is possible in the short run. Risk and reward should be in balance. Although the needs of the organization as a whole must be paramount, the needs of its parts shouldn't be neglected. All the requirements that organizations have should be considered, and balanced – system, culture, leadership and power.

- **Courage**

  Downgrading hierarchy will nearly always mean upsetting powerful people. This takes guts. I am not recommending a headlong attack, rather the sustained exercise of the leadership potential that people have across all organizations. Hierarchy is always political, however it may be dressed up.

Hierarchy will not easily withdraw. Understanding, inventiveness, balance and bravery will be needed to shift it.

Hierarchy will not easily withdraw. Understanding, inventiveness, balance and bravery will be needed to shift it. But there is good reason to hope that it can be shifted. Vast energy presently goes into propping up hierarchy. Releasing this energy for constructive use will bring great and clearly recognizable benefits. It will allow organizations to emerge that are much more effective for getting things done and much better places in which to work. There are strong instrumental reasons (relating to effectiveness) and strong moral reasons (relating to the better use of human potential) for exploring a radical shift away from hierarchy in organizations of all types. To do this, let us summon up our energy, courage and organizational imagination.

Glossary

Autonomy – see Responsible autonomy

Bureaucracy

Originally from the French: bureau = desk and, later, office; + the Greek suffix: -kratia = power of. Popular use is for cumbersome procedures ('red tape') and self-serving administration. Organizational theory follows Max Weber: administrative staff members have clearly defined duties and powers, separate from their personal lives, in a strict hierarchy and following carefully defined rules, which enable decentralization. Weber also stresses professionalism of bureaucrats (Weber 1920/1964)

Sections 3.2, 7.2

Co-evolution

Co-evolution happens when the evolution of something is influenced by the evolution of other things. The emphasis is on the reciprocal interaction of a series of elements within an ecosystem. Maturana gives the example of wearing a new pair of shoes – both your feet and the shoes change to accommodate each other (Mitleton-Kelly 2003). Co-evolution is distinguished from adaptation of an element to an external environment, when only the element is considered to change, not the environment.

Section 5.4

Complex evolving system (CES)

Complex behaviour arises from the intricate intertwining or inter-connectivity of elements within a system (Mitleton-Kelly 2003). Individuals or elements in a CES, following their own agendas or even acting at random, can create new order and coherence, without any grand design determining their actions. A CES is therefore capable of evolving new forms and capabilities, spontaneously and over time.

Section 4.4

Contingency theory

Contingency theory holds that organizations are fully effective only when their internal structures, procedures and cultures are suited to the contingencies or circumstances they encounter. Organizations are shaped by contingencies, because they need to adapt to them in order to avoid loss of performance. In other words, contingencies determine organizational characteristics. Contingency theory is particularly concerned with the stability of organizations' markets, their technological environments, their size and their strategy (Donaldson 2001)

Sections 7.1, 7.2, 7.4

Critique

The root word is Greek: kritos = a judge. For organizations, the term means the evaluation or appraisal of the performance of autonomous sub-units against a variety of criteria. Critique includes audit, financial analysis, social and environmental accountability. It requires clearly defined criteria and regular review.

Sections 4.6, 5.7, 8.16

Cultural theory

Cultural theory (Thompson, Ellis and Wildavsky 1990) was developed out of Mary Douglas's Grid and Group typology (Douglas 1982). It describes individualism, hierarchy and egalitarianism as the three active ways of life in society and postulates a dynamic equilibrium between the three ways, which is to the advantage of societies in which they are combined. Triarchy theory relates to organizations rather than to societies. But there are parallels between the two theories: individualism corresponds to responsible autonomy; egalitarianism corresponds to heterarchy; and both theories refer to hierarchy.

Sections 6.1, 6.2, 6.3

Culture

The culture of an organization is the way it works. It includes the shared assumptions of the organization's members, often tacit rather than explicit, and the values, language and mental models they share. Raymond Williams writes that culture is one of the most complicated words in English (Williams 1976). It can mean growing things (e.g. agriculture) and hence human development. It can mean refinement or taste. And it can mean a particular way of life. The last meaning is the one most relevant for the study of organizations.

Section 3.3

Democracy

The root words are Greek: demos = people, kratos = rule. Political theory distinguishes between representative democracy (the election of representatives, who then make decisions) and direct democracy (decisions made at a town meeting or by referendum). In organizations, the term can mean actions that are non-authoritarian, consultative, and respectful of everyone's rights and opinions. It can also mean decision-making by voting, e.g. in professional partnerships. The latter is the meaning preferred in this book.

Sections 5.2, 7.3, 8.4, 8.15

Encapsulation

Amitai Etzioni uses the term for the societal process that allows markets to flourish. A capsule is created within which market interactions take place. Examples of institutions that create the capsule are: laws that enforce contracts, protect property and prevent deception and corruption; legal incorporation of limited liability companies, with a requirement for regular and accurate reporting; well-regulated and open stock and commodity exchanges; and means for resolution of disputes. In this book, I adapt the term to mean the procedures and rules within organizations that create the conditions for responsible autonomy of certain sub-units. Some of the procedures will be like those in society; others will be specific to organizations.

Sections 4.5, 4.7, 8.16.

Getting things done

A term originally used by the Coverdale Organization to mean purposive action, such as performing an organizational function, defining or carrying out tasks. The things that are done in an organization should, of course, be those that further the organization's purpose.

Section 3.1

Heterarchy

The root words are Greek: hetero = different, kratos= rule. The term was introduced into social science by James Ogilvy. It means multiple or dispersed rule. Heterarchy has a balance of powers rather than the single rule of hierarchy. No one person or group is dominant. Decisions are reached by dialogue rather than by dictat. Influence varies according to the matter being considered and also varies over time. Heterarchy is what happens in everyday interactions between individuals and groups when they are conducted on a basis of reasonable equality.

Sections 4.2, 4.8, 5.2, 6.2, 7.2, 8.12, 8.15

Hierarchy

Hierarchy originally meant rule by a priesthood, and the term was also used to refer to the ranks of heavenly beings, such as angels and archangels. Hierarchy today refers to rule by a single, supreme ruler, whose will controls a society or an organization. The supreme ruler passes authority on to a series of lesser rulers, and so on, down through a pyramid. Because it starts with a single ruler we can call hierarchy 'single rule', as opposed to the multiple rule of heterarchy.

Sections 4.1, 5.1, 6.2, 7.2, 7.5, 8.2, 9.9

Hegemony

The term derives from the Greek: hegemon = ruler, often an alien ruler. Its use today is mostly that of Antonio Gramsci, who did not limit its use to direct political control, but used it to describe an overall dominance, leading to enduring ways of seeing the world which are accepted as normal by most people, because they have grown up with these ways and feel it would be absurd to doubt or question them.

Sections 1.1, 2.1

Leadership

In organization theory, the term leader was traditionally used to refer to someone (usually officially appointed) who influences, and sometimes inspires, a group or organization in its choice of goals and in their achievement. The concept has since been widened to include sense-making on behalf of a group, the promotion of particular values in a group, and a symbolic role. The idea of 'dispersed leadership' moves the focus from heroic individuals towards the development of everyone's leadership capabilities. A leader is then seen as a sense-maker and facilitator, although inspiration remains important in some situations.

Sections 3.4, 8.7, 9.3

Management

The word appears to have two separate roots: management = handling (c.f. Manipulate) and management = good housekeeping (French: ménage). Two meanings remain. On one hand, 'the management' means those in power in an organization, those who define tasks for others, or those who control others (in contrast to the workers, who carry out tasks defined by managers). On the other hand, management is an activity (preferably a competent one), performed in organizations and in daily life. Management is sometimes contrasted with leadership, the latter being inspirational and the former more mundane.

Sections 3.6, 8.2

Network

The metaphor of the net, a highly flexible structure with cords and nodes, suggests that mutual influence and communication are spread out in space.

Networking is the exchange of information and influence, in a loosely-coupled, cellular structure, which may be completely informal or partly formalized and facilitated. Manuel Castells writes that our societies are increasingly structured around a bipolar opposition between the self and the net. Networking often depends on electronic technology but is primarily a social phenomenon. A network is predominately a heterarchy, but one without a strong common purpose, which is what an organizational heterarchy should have.

Section 4.2

Organization

The root word is Greek: organon = tool or instrument. Today, the meaning of organization, as an entity, is a group of people working together for some purpose. Organization is also an activity, and here the meaning relates to the creation of discipline and order.

Sections 2.3, 3.1, 3.3, 3.4, 3.5, 3.6, 3.7

The Three Ways of Getting Things Done

Plasticity

Roberto Unger (Unger 1987) uses the term plasticity to explain how work relations within an organization can be "constantly shifted in order to suit changing circumstances". Unger emphasizes the need to facilitate movement away from hierarchy, and to experiment with alternative ways of getting things done. He suggests that plasticity has increased with two factors: a reduction in the distinction between task-definition and task-execution (those who manage and those who do the work) and the softening of established social roles and hierarchies in society as a whole (which promotes plasticity within that society's organizations).

Section 8.14

Pluralism

In society, pluralism means the existence and toleration of a variety of groups with different ethnic origins, cultures or religions. In organizations, pluralism means valuing individual diversity, whether ethnic or of personal characteristics and skills. An organization can have a strong culture, with a common purpose and shared values, language and mental models, while at the same time seeking pluralism and diversity among its members.

Section 5.5

Power

Power is necessary to mobilize action. Stewart Clegg argues that power is central to organization and organization is central to power (Clegg 1989). In his view, power is dynamic, being rather like a game. Power arises neither from the individual wills of powerful people nor from social structures but from interactions, usually complex ones. In hierarchies, power depends a lot on threats and inducements. In heterarchies, it depends mainly on persuasion and mutual benefit or mutual obligations. Power in organizations is often concealed, which obscures both the necessity of power in getting things done and the danger that power will corrupt.

Section 3.5

Responsible autonomy

Autonomy is self-government, self-organization or the absence of external rule. Autonomy is to be contrasted with hierarchy's single rule and heterarchy's multiple rule. For autonomy to become responsible autonomy, the absence of external rule must not mean there is no accountability for the outcome of self-organization. With responsible autonomy, the ways in which outcomes are achieved are not externally controlled, but the outcomes are monitored and poor outcomes are sanctioned.

Sections 4.3, 4.6, 4.8, 5.7, 6.2, 7.2, 8.16

Separation of powers

This is a term taken from political science, where it means the division or balance of powers and responsibilities within a state. A well-known separation is that between the executive, legislative and judicial functions of government. In a federal state, there is also a separation of powers between the federal level and the level of States (USA), Länder (Germany) or Provinces (Canada). In organizations, it means a split of responsibilities and authority between staff and line functions or between central and peripheral units.

Sections 4.2, 8.5

System

Collins Dictionary gives eleven different meanings for 'system', but these fall into two main groups. The meaning of the first group is an orderly way of doing things or of communicating information – today this is often a computerized system. The relevant adjective is 'systematic'. The meaning of the second group is an entity which, to be properly understood, has to be considered as a whole. For this kind of system, the whole is different from the sum of its parts or, to put it another way, the system is seen to have emergent properties (Checkland 1999). Here the relevant adjective is 'systemic'.

Section 3.2

The three ways

The three ways of getting things done in organizations are: hierarchy, heterarchy and responsible autonomy.

Sections 3.1, 4.10

Triarchy

The combination of the three ways is called triarchy, or triple rule. The study of the workings of organizational triarchies is called triarchics.

Notes

Section

1.1   Peter Senge and Margaret Wheatley – 'Changing How We Work Together' 2002. See also Senge – *The Fifth Discipline* 1990, pp. 181-6.

Rosabeth Moss Kanter – *The Change Masters* 1983, p. 257.

1.2   James Ogilvy – 'What Sartre Can Teach Strategists' 2004, p. 6.

1.3   Matt Ridley – *The Origins of Virtue* 1996, p. 157.

Anthony Stevens and John Price – *Evolutionary Psychiatry* 1996, p. 25.

See also Nigel Nicholson, *Managing the Human Animal* 2002. As far as I know, Nicholson's book was the first major use of evolutionary psychology in the analysis of organizational functions. Nicholson believes that hierarchy is inevitable, that it is a myth that we can create non-hierarchical organizations (p. 30). However, he also writes: "We have become addicted to hierarchical structures – or rather, we have lost sight of the alternative, the fluid, decentralized status order of the hunter-gatherer clan, which is not non-hierarchical but egalitarian in spirit and function." (p. 256).

2.4   Leo Tolstoy – Second epilogue, *War and Peace* 1896/1975, p. 1416.

2.5   Thomas Hobbes – *Leviathan* 1651/1962, p. 66.

Max Weber – *The Theory of Social and Economic Organization*, 1920/1964, p. 146, p. 328.

3.2   Paul Adler and Bryan Borys – 'Two Types of Bureaucracy: Enabling and Coercive' 1996.

3.4   Jim Collins – *Great to Good* 2001.

Karl Weick – *Sense-making in Organizations* 1995.

Dispersed Leadership – see A. Bryman 'Leadership in Organizations' 1996.

3.5   For more about power, see Cynthia Hardy and Stewart Clegg's essay, 'Some Dare Call It Power' in Clegg, Hardy and Nord, *The Handbook of Organization Studies* 1996, pp. 622–641. The essay takes its title from the epigram of Sir John Harington (1561–1612):

Treason doth never prosper: what's the reason?
For if it prosper, none dare call it treason.

The thesis of Hardy and Clegg is that explicit or implicit pressure from the powerful stops most consideration around the nature of power, leaving it a poorly understood factor in organizational life. They advocate the questioning of our inherited values, so that we "become more aware of how we are also prisoners in a web of power that we have helped to create". See also Clegg's excellent book *Frameworks of Power* 1998.

3.6   Albert Hirschman – *Exit, Voice and Loyalty* 1970.

4.1   Weber 1920/1964 p. 146.

4.2   Since it may be a novel term to many readers, and as it is central to this book, I will describe some of the history of the concept of heterarchy. James Ogilvy writes, "Back in the late seventies, in a book about decentralization, I borrowed from the biologist, Warren McCulloch, an ungainly word – heterarchy – and introduced it into the discourse on the governance of large corporations." (Ogilvy's Foreword in Fairtlough 1994). Ogilvy's book about decentralization is *Many Dimensional Man* 1977 and his source for McCulloch's ideas is the latter's *Embodiments of Mind* 1965. For Ogilvy, "Heterarchy represents a balance between the need for some hierarchy, combined with the need for the lateral, horizontal links in a network of relationships." (Fairtlough 1994).

In 1979, Ogilvy developed the concept of heterarchy in a paper written together with Peter Schwartz, who was then his colleague at SRI International, the Californian consultancy company (Schwartz and Ogilvy 1979). Later, in the early 1980s, Ogilvy collaborated with Donald Michael in a series of workshops on the topic 'Making Heterarchy Work', which were summed up in a paper by Michael entitled 'Neither Hierarchy nor Anarchy: Notes on Norms for Governance in a Systemic World' 1983. The use of the term in my book *Creative Compartments* (Fairtlough 1994) followed the Ogilvy/Michael tradition by describing heterarchy as leadership of a mixed or distributed kind, in which responsibility and authority are shared by everybody.

The originator of the concept is sometimes said to be Gregory Bateson. In his well-known book *Steps to an Ecology of Mind* 1972, he develops a theory of human learning, in which 'orders' of learning are ranked from the simplest reaction to a signal, through learning to react to new signals, to learning how to learn, and finally to long-term improvements in learning to learn. In this book, Bateson describes these orders of learning as a hierarchy. But later, in his *Mind and Nature* 1979, he uses 'heterarchy' to describe the interrelation of orders. He abandoned the term hierarchy because of the implication it carries of higher orders exercising control over, or being more important than, lower ones. Bateson's theory concerned the learning of individuals. Other authors applied his ideas to organizational learning, also preferring the term 'heterarchy' in this context.

In the mid-1980s, Gunnar Hedlund developed the concept of heterarchy in a series of papers on the multinational corporation (MNC) (Hedlund 1986, 1993). He distinguishes heterarchy from hierarchy using a range of features. Hedlund says that the concept of heterarchy captures "the decentralized strategic control, laterality of contacts and learning orientation of the advanced, modern MNC." (1993). A particularly important feature is 'normative control', meaning that people throughout an organization are socialized into adopting a vision of the organization's purpose and sharing its values. They are guided by vision and values rather than by hierarchical command and control.

Another feature noted by Hedlund is lateral linkage between multiple centres in an MNC. The responsibilities of these centres shift over time, which generates flows of products, people and knowledge between them, often without the involvement of the MNC's headquarters. Hedlund's ideas were taken up by Ikujiro Nonaka and Hirotaka Takeuchi, who found them useful in describing the way Japanese corporations work. (Hedlund and Nonaka 1993, Nonaka and Takeuchi 1995).

4.3   Adam Smith – *The Wealth of Nations* 1776/1986.

4.4   Eve Mitleton-Kelly is a leading exponent of ideas from complexity thinking as they relate to organizations. She identifies strands of thinking in the natural and social sciences that, during the 1990s, came together to generate a "conceptual framework, a way of thinking, and a way of seeing the world." (Mitleton-Kelly – *Complex Systems and Evolutionary Perspectives on Organisations* 2003, p. 26, original emphasis removed.) I would add a further source of ideas for complexity theory: systems thinking. (Peter Checkland – *Systems Thinking, Systems Practice* 1981/1999).

Self-organization, emergence, connectivity, far-from-equilibrium, co-evolution, path-dependence and the creation of new order are some of the ideas involved in complexity thinking. A very productive source of complexity ideas has been the Santa Fe Institute in New Mexico from which emerged the concept of a Complex Adaptive System (Holland 1995, Kauffman 1995). I agree with Mitleton-Kelly in preferring the term Complex Evolving Systems (CESs). Lately, she has modified the term to Complex Co-Evolving Systems (CCESs), which might be better still (personal communication, 2005).

Complexity thinking relates both to heterarchy and responsible autonomy. Connectivity, interdependence and co-evolution particularly relate to heterarchy; self-organization, emergence and CES particularly relate to responsible autonomy.

4.5   Amitai Etzioni – *The Moral Dimension* 1988.

4.6   The concept of critique was developed in Chapter 9 of my book *Creative Compartments* (Fairtlough 1994). To a limited extent, my thinking was influenced by critical theory's aim of uncovering society's unquestioned assumptions. But as I use the term, critique applies to organizations, and is a process of evaluation of the performance of an autonomous unit. It can be looked at as a combination of Hirschman's Exit and Voice. 'Exit' relates to the automatic kind of critique provided for business firms by the market, and for membership organizations by their failure to recruit or retain their members. 'Voice' relates to an informed appraisal of the unit, and to the expression of the results as constructive feedback to the unit. As I wrote: "Stringent, but sympathetic, critique can help us all, so we should set about organizing it for ourselves, if we don't already have it." (Fairtlough 1994, p. 168).

5.1 Hobbes 1651/1962.

5.3 Robert Axelrod – *The Evolution of Co-operation* 1990.

5.4 Mitleton-Kelly 2003.

5.6 Meredith Belbin's work is described in Peter Jay, 'Nobody's Perfect – but a team can be' 1980.

Edward Roberts and Alan Fusfeld – 'Staffing the Innovative Technology-Based Organization' 1981.

Kate Hopkinson is the founder of the Inner Skills organization. Her analysis is taken from a presentation at the London School of Economics, July 2004, entitled 'Landscape of the Mind: a Fresh Way of Unfurling Human Potential' and from a subsequent personal communication. For further information see www.innerskills.co.uk or e-mail hopkinson@innerskills.co.uk.

6.1 Michael Thompson, Richard Ellis and Aaron Wildavsky – *Cultural Theory* 1990.

6.2 Thompson *et al* 1990.

7.2 Lex Donaldson – *The Contingency Theory of Organizations* 2001.

Tom Burns and G. M. Stalker – *The Management of Innovation* 1961.

Henry Mintzberg – *The Structuring of Organizations* 1971.

Initiated by Meyer and Rowan in 1977 (Scott and Meyer 1994), the area within organization studies known as Institutional Theory is based on the insight that the structure of an organization has symbolic meaning, both to its members and to the outside world. (Tolbert and Zucker in Clegg, Hardy and Nord, p. 177). "Organizations reflect patterns or templates established in a wider system… School, firm, or hospital structures reflect standard forms created in the wider environment." (Scott and Meyer 1994, p .2). Drawing to some extent on Jungian thinking, Greenwood and Hinings (1993) call such widely accepted structures 'archetypes'. Copying what has worked for others, or is familiar, or has some external legitimation, may well mean that an organization's arrangements (like those of the psyche) do not fit particularly well with its actual needs. Thus, the hegemony of hierarchy in a particular organization is strongly reinforced by what happens outside it. Institutional Theory is therefore opposed, to some extent, to Contingency Theory.

A typology with some similarities to that of Donaldson has been developed by Max Boisot and John Child (1988). It relates to the coordination of activities in society. They start by distinguishing between modes of coordination that depend on impersonal, codified, explicit information and those that use personalized, flexible, tacit information. They give as an example of codified information the worldwide transmission of variations in the Dow Jones index of stock prices – achieved in seconds, and just as rapidly understood by anyone interested in such matters, whatever language they speak. At the opposite, uncodified extreme, their example is the mastery of arcane Zen practices, which may take half a lifetime to learn, even for acolytes living closely with the Zen master.

Boisot and Child go on to distinguish between open information, like the Dow Jones, which is available to everyone, and secret information, known only to insiders. Coordination through open, codified information they describe as 'market' coordination. When coordination uses secretive, codified information, they call it 'hierarchical' coordination.

Open, uncodified information results in 'clan' coordination, while secret, uncodified information produces coordination by 'fief'. The fief is like a mediaeval village, under the feudal system, with the Lord of the Manor in charge. They compare the clan to a primaeval, democratic, hunter-gatherer band.

Market	*Hierarchy*
Impersonal, open	Impersonal, secretive
Clan	*Fief*
Personal, open	Personal, secretive

Although the Boisot-Child model is thought-provoking, it applies to whole societies. For organizations, I think a different analysis is needed. I also think that power, as well as information flow, needs to be considered – although as the saying 'knowledge is power' implies, the two are connected.

Taking into account their power-relations, I would class the Boisot/Child fiefs as primarily hierarchical, although they are not the classic bureaucratic hierarchies of Max Weber. The mode of coordination that Boisot and Child call the clan is predominantly heterarchical.

Responsible autonomy can involve an internal market within an organization, but trading is not the only possible relationship between an organization's autonomous units. Therefore, 'market' is not the right term to describe the operation of responsible autonomy *within* an organization.

If centralization of decision-making can be equated with secrecy, and if personal/impersonal is equivalent to formal/informal, then the Donaldson model of organization styles translates into the Boisot/Child model of societal coordination. This isn't surprising, since both models centre on information, communication and knowledge. (Both system and culture are, to a large extent, sediments of shared knowledge.) See also Fairtlough 1994, Chapter 7.

7.3   Thomas Malone – *The Future of Work* 2003, p. 49. See also Malone, Laubacher and Morton *Inventing the Organizations of the 21st Century* 2003.

Russell Ackoff has talked wisely and wittily about many of the issues raised in this book, including managers' views of internal and external markets. His most recent book is *Management f-Laws* 2007.

7.5 Jane Jacobs – *Systems of Survival* 1992.

Williamson Murray – 'May 1940' 2001.

See also Alistair Horne's *To Lose a Battle* 1969. For further examples of military hierarchy in action, see Eliot Cohen's and John Gooch's *Military Misfortunes* 1990.

7.6 Fairtlough 1994.

Robin Dunbar – *Grooming, Gossip, and the Evolution of Language* 1996.

8.2 Gustave Flaubert, in a letter to Louise Colet, 1833.

Kenneth Cloke and Joan Goldsmith – *The End of Management* 2002.

8.3 David Bohm – *Wholeness and the Implicate Order* 1983.

Another valuable skill relates to the resolution of dilemmas, arising when two of a group's firmly held values are in conflict over a particular issue. Charles Hampden-Turner, in *Corporate Culture* 1990, proposes that in such cases the situation should be viewed in a wider frame of reference. The process of reframing needs both communication skills and skill in conceptualization.

Regarding teamwork, see Hackman, *Leading Teams* 2002.

8.4 Malone 2004.

Lorsch and Tierney – *Aligning the Stars* 2002.

8.7 Nonaka and Takeuchi 1995.

8.8 Aristotle – *The Athenian Constitution* 1984.

8.10 Ricardo Semler – *Maverick* 2003 and *The Seven-Day Weekend* 2003.

See also Nicholson 2000, pp. 33-37.

Fairtlough 1994.

8.11 Mitleton-Kelly 2003.

8.13 Sally Bibb and Jeremy Kourdi – *Trust Matters for Organisational and Personal Success* 2004.

Fairtlough 1994.

8.14 Roberto Unger – *Plasticity into Power* 1987.

8.16 Mitleton-Kelly 2003.

W. Edwards Deming – *Out of the Crisis* 2000. Deming is often referred to as the father of Total Quality Management and his approach to management was primarily concerned with improving organizational systems and processes. Although his 14 points implicitly call into question many of the assumptions that underlie hierarchical management structures, he did not, as far as I know, use the term heterarchy.

9.1 The first volume of the three-volume work by Manuel Castells on the Information Age, is entitled *The Rise of the Network Society*. He writes: "A network-based social structure is a highly dynamic, open system, susceptible to innovating without threatening its balance" (Castells 1996, p. 470). This suggests that, in a network society, heterarchy will more easily find its place.

To add to the sociological insights of Castells, see Freeman and Louça *As Time Goes By* 2001 for insights on the evolution of technology and its profound economic effects. For political insights, see Philip Bobbitt's *The Shield of Achilles* 2002, in which he describes the evolution of the nation-state into 'the market state'. Robert Cooper in *The Breaking of Nations* 2003 calls this new form 'the postmodern state', which seems to me a better term. It is evident from works like these that the social, technological, economic and political aspects of society co-evolve with blends of the three ways used by society's organizations to get things done.

9.3   John Roberts – *The Modern Firm* 2004.

Bibliography

Ackoff, Russell L., Addison, Herbert J. and Bibb, Sally. *Management f-Laws: How organizations really work*. Axminster: Triarchy Press, 2007.

Aristotle. *The Athenian Constitution*, trans P. J. Rhodes, London: Penguin, 1984.

Axelrod, Robert. *The Evolution of Cooperation*. London: Penguin, 1990.

Adler, Paul S. and Borys, Bryan. 'Two Types of Bureaucracy: Enabling and Coercive', *Administrative Science Quarterly*, Vol 41, 61, 1996.

Bateson, Gregory. *Steps to an Ecology of Mind*. London: Paladin, 1972.

Belbin, R. Meredith. *Management Teams: Why They Succeed or Fail*. London: Heinemann, 1981.

-- *Mind and Nature: A Necessary Unity*. New York: Dutton, 1979.

Bibb, Sally and Kourdi, Jeremy. *Trust Matters for Organisational and Personal Success*. Basingstoke: Palgrave Macmillan, 2004.

Bobbitt, Philip. *The Shield of Achilles: War, Peace and the Course of History*. New York: Alfred A. Knopf, 2002.

Bohm, David. *Wholeness and the Implicate Order*. New York: Harper Rowe, 1983.

Boisot, Max and Child, John. 'The Iron Law of Fiefs: Bureaucratic Failure and the Problem of Governance in the Chinese Economic Reforms'. *Administrative Science Quarterly*, Vol. 33, 1988, pp. 507-527.

Bryman, A. 'Leadership in Organizations'. *Organization Studies*. Clegg, Stewart R., Hardy, Cynthia and Nord, Walter R., ed. London: Sage, 1996, pp. 283-4.

Burns, Tom and Stalker, G. M. *The Management of Innovation*. London: Tavistock, 1961.

Castells, Manuel. *The Rise of the Network Society: The Information Age: Economy, Society and Culture*. Volume 1. Oxford: Blackwells, 1996.

Checkland, Peter. *Systems Thinking, Systems Practice*. (1981) Chichester: John Wiley & Sons, 1999.

Clegg, Stewart. *Frameworks of Power*. London: Sage, 1998.

Clegg, Stewart and Kornberger, Martin. *Managing and Organizations: An Introduction to Theory and Practice*. London: Sage Publications, 2004.

Clegg, Stewart, Courpasson, David and Phillips, Nelson. *Power and Organizations.* London: Sage Publications, 2006.

Cloke, Kenneth and Goldsmith, Joan. *The End of Management and the Rise of Organizational Democracy.* San Francisco: Jossey-Bass, 2002.

Cohen, Eliot A. and Gooch, John. *Military Misfortunes: the Anatomy of Failure in War.* London: Free Press, 1990.

Collins, Jim. *Good to Great: Why Some Companies Make the Leap and Others Don't.* London: Random House, 2001.

Cooper, Robert. *The Breaking of Nations: Order and Chaos in the Twenty-first Century.* London: Atlantic, 2003.

Deming, W. Edwards. *Out of the Crisis.* Cambridge, MA: MIT Press, 2000.

Donaldson, Lex. *The Contingency Theory of Organizations.* London: Sage, 2001.

Douglas, Mary. 'Introduction to Grid/Group Analysis'. *Essays in the Sociology of Perception.* Douglas, M. ed. Boston: Routledge & Kegan Paul, 1982.

Dunbar, Robin. *Grooming, Gossip and the Evolution of Language.* London: Faber & Faber, 1996.

Etzioni, Amitai. *The Moral Dimension: Towards a New Economics.* London: Collier Macmillan, 1988.

Fairtlough, Gerard. *Creative Compartments: A Design for Future Organisation.* London: Adamantine, 1994.

Freeman, C. and Louçã, F. *As Time Goes By: from the Industrial Revolutions to the Information Revolution.* Oxford: Oxford University Press, 2001.

Greenwood, Royston and Hinings, C. K. 'Understanding Strategic Change: The Contribution of Archetypes' *Academy of Management Journal*, Vol. 36, No. 5, 1993, pp. 1052–1081

Hackman, J. Richard. *Leading Teams: Setting the Stage for Great Performances.* Boston, MA: Harvard Business School Press, 2002.

Hampden-Turner, Charles. *Corporate Culture: From Vicious Circles to Virtuous Circles.* London: Hutchinson, 1990.

Hardy, Cynthia and Clegg, Stewart. 'Some Dare Call It Power' in Clegg, Stewart R., Hardy, Cynthia, Nord, Walter R., eds. *The Handbook of Organization Studies.* London: Sage, 1996, pp. 622–641.

Hedlund, Gunnar. 'The Hypermodern MNC – A Heterarchy?' *Human Resource Management*, 25, no. 1, 1986, pp. 9-35.

-- 'Managing the MNC: The End of the Missionary Era' in *Organization of Transnational Corporations*. Gunnar Hedlund, ed. London: Routledge, 1993.

Hedlund, Gunnar and Nonaka, Ikujiro. 'Models of Knowledge: Management in the West and Japan' in *Implementing Strategic Process: Change, Learning and Cooperation*. Lorange, P. et al. eds. Oxford: Basil Blackwell, 1993, pp. 117–144.

Hirschman, Albert O. *Exit, Voice, and Loyalty: Responses to Decline in Firms, Organizations, and States*. Cambridge, MA & London: Harvard University Press, 1970.

Hobbes, Thomas. *Leviathan, or the Matter, Form, and Power of a Commonwealth, Ecclesiastical and Civil*. (1651). Everyman edition. London: J. M. Dent & Sons, 1962.

Holland, John H. *Hidden Order: How Adaptation Builds Complexity*. Reading, MA: Helix Books, Addison-Wesley Publishing, 1995.

Jacobs, Jane. *Systems of Survival: a Dialogue on the Moral Foundation of Commerce and Politics*. London: Hodder & Stoughton, 1992.

Jay, Peter. 'Nobody's Perfect – but a team can be' *Observer Magazine*. 20.4.1980, pp. 25–38.

Kanter, Rosabeth Moss. *The Change Masters: Corporate Entrepreneurs at Work*. London: George Allen & Unwin, 1983.

Kauffman, Stuart A. *At Home in the Universe: The Search for the Laws of Self-Organization and Complexity*. London: Penguin, 1995.

Lorsch, Jay W. and Tierney, Thomas J. *Aligning the Stars: How to Succeed When Professionals Drive Results*. Boston, MA: Harvard Business School Press, 2002.

McCulloch, Warren S. *Embodiments of Mind*. Cambridge, MA: MIT Press, 1965.

Malone, Thomas. *The Future of Work: How the New Order of Business Will Shape Your Organization, Your Management Style, and Your Life*. Boston, MA: Harvard Business School Press, 2004.

Malone, Thomas, Laubacher, Robert and Scott Morton, Michael S. *Inventing the Organizations of the 21st Century*. Cambridge, MA & London: MIT Press, 2003.

Maturana, Humberto R. and Varela, Francisco J. *Autopoeisis and Cognition: The Realization of the Living*. Dordrecht: D. Reidel, 1980.

Meyer, J. W. and Rowan, B. 'Institutionalized Organizations: Formal Structure as Myth and Ceremony'. *American Journal of Sociology*, No. 83, 1977, pp. 340–363.

Michael, Donald. *Learning to Plan – And Planning to Learn*. San Francisco, Washington, London: Jossey-Bass, 1973.

-- 'Neither Hierarchy nor Anarchy: Notes on Norms for Governance in a Systematic World' in *Rethinking Liberalism,* W. T. Anderson, ed. New York: Avon, 1983.

Mintzberg, Henry. *The Structuring of Organizations: A Synthesis of the Research.* Englewood Cliffs, NJ: Prentice Hall, 1979.

Mitleton-Kelly, Eve. *Complex Systems and Evolutionary Perspectives of Organisations: The Application of Complexity Theory to Organisations.* Oxford: Elsevier Science, 2003.

Mitleton-Kelly, Eve. 'The Information Systems Professional as a Hermit'. Innovation: *The European Journal of Social Science Research*, Vol 17. No 4, 2004, p. 289.

Murray, Williamson. 'May 1940: Contingency and Fragility of the German RMA' in Knox, MacGregor, Murray, Williamson, *The Dynamics of Military Revolution 1300– 2050*, Cambridge: Cambridge University Press, 2001.

Nicholson, N. *Managing the Human Animal*. London: Texere, 2002.

Nonaka, Ikujiro and Takeuki, Hirotaka. *The Knowledge-Creating Company: How Japanese Companies Create the Dynamics of Innovation*. New York & London: Oxford University Press, 1995.

Ogilvy, James. 'What Sartre Can Teach Strategists'. *Strategy and Business*, Issue 33, 2004, p. 6.

-- *Many Dimensional Man: Decentralizing Self, Society, and the Sacred.* New York: Oxford University Press, 1977.

Ridley, Matt. *The Origins of Virtue*. London: Viking, 1996.

Roberts, Edward B. and Fusfeld, Alan R. 'Staffing the Innovative Technology-Based Organization'. *Sloan Management Review*, Spring, 1981, pp. 19–34.

Roberts, John. *The Modern Firm*. Oxford: Oxford University Press, 2004.

Schwartz, Peter and Ogilvy, James. 'The Emergent Paradigm: Changing Patterns of Thought and Belief' Analytical Report, *Values and Lifestyles Program*, April 1979.

Scott, W. Richard, Meyer, John W. et al. *Institutional Environments and Organizations: Structural Complexity and Individualism*. London: Sage, 1994.

Semler, Ricardo. *Maverick: The Success Story Behind the World's Most Unusual Workplace*. New York: Warner Books, 2003.

-- *The Seven-Day Weekend: The Wisdom Revolution: Finding the Work/Life Balance*. London: Century, 2003.

Senge, Peter. *The Fifth Discipline: The Art and Practice of the Learning Organization*. London: Century Business, 1992.

Senge, Peter and Wheatley, Margaret. 'Changing How We Work Together' *Reflections: The SOL Journal* Spring, 2002, pp. 63–67.

Smith, Adam. *The Wealth of Nations 1–3*. (1776). London: Penguin, 1986.

Stevens, Anthony and Price, John. *Evolutionary Psychiatry: A New Beginning*. London: Routledge, 1996.

Thompson, Michael, Ellis, Richard and Wildavsky, Aaron. *Cultural Theory*. Boulder, CO: Westview Press, 1990.

Tolbert, Pamela S. and Zucker, Lynne G. 'The Institutionalization of Institutional Theory' in *The Handbook of Organization Studies*. Clegg, Stewart R., Hardy, Cynthia, Nord, Walter R., eds. London: Sage, 1996, pp. 175–190.

Tolstoy, Leo. *War and Peace*. (1869). Harmondsworth: Penguin, 1975.

Unger, Roberto. *Plasticity into Power: Variations on Themes of Politics: A Work in Constructive Social Theory*. Cambridge: Cambridge University Press, 1987.

Weber, Max. *The Theory of Social and Economic Organization*. (1920) Trans. A. M. Henderson & Talcott Parsons. Free Press Edition. New York: Simon & Schuster, 1964.

Weick, Karl. *Sensemaking in Organizations*. Thousand Oaks, CA and London: Sage, 1995.

Williams, Raymond. *Keywords: A Vocabulary of Culture and Society*. London: Fontana, 1983.

About Triarchy Press

Triarchy Press is a new publishing house that looks at how organizations work and how to make them work better. We aim to present challenging perspectives on organizations in short, pithy, but rigorously argued, books.

In addition to providing us with our first publication project, Gerard Fairtlough's *The Three Ways of Getting Things Done* has been inspirational to our organization from its conception - and continues to influence our day-to-day interactions. While the balance between hierarchy, heterarchy and responsible autonomy constantly shifts in our living company, the struggle to challenge hegemonies, to maintain a pioneering intellectual spirit and to practice what we preach has so far proved immensely rewarding for Triarchy Press - and for the individuals involved with the company and its expanding list of projects.

Through our books, e-publications and discussion area, we aim to stimulate ideas by encouraging real debate about organizations in partnership with people who work in them, research them or just like to think about them.

To submit an article or book proposal, to join the discussion or to find out more about us, please visit our website:

www.triarchypress.com

Biography of the Author

Gerard Fairtlough was trained as a biochemist, graduating from Cambridge University in 1953. He worked in the Royal Dutch/Shell group for 25 years, the last five as CEO of Shell Chemicals UK. In 1980, he founded the leading biopharmaceuticals company Celltech and was its CEO until 1990. Since then, he has been involved in the start-up of several high-technology businesses, as a non-executive director or as a 'business angel'.

He has been an advisor to various government and academic institutions, including Specialist Advisor to the House of Commons Select Committee on Science and Technology, a member of the Science and Engineering Research Council and Chair of the Advisory Panel, Science Policy Research Unit, Sussex University.

Gerard is the author of *Creative Compartments: A Design for Future Organisation* (London: Adamantine Press, 1994), co-author with Julie Allan and Barbara Heinzen of *The Power of the Tale: Using Narratives for Organisational Success* (Chichester: Wiley, 2001) and *New York Changed My Life; A Memoir of the 1960s* (2004). He has also written extensively on the theory and practice of organizations and of innovation.

Printed in the United Kingdom
by Lightning Source UK Ltd.
119396UK00001B/383-488